The Dramatically Different Classroom

Multiple Intelligences Activities Across the Curriculum

Christine Laitta
& Mark Weakland

Kagan

Kagan Publishing
1160 Calle Cordillera
San Clemente, CA 92673
1(800) WEE CO-OP
www.KaganOnline.com

ISBN: 1-879097-67-2

Table of Contents

Creating the Ensemble

Language Arts

Social Studies

Mathematics

iv

The Dramatically Different Classroom • Christine Laitta & Mark Weakland
Kagan Publishing • 1 (800) WEE CO-OP • www.KaganOnline.com

Science & Health

Taking a Break

Chart of Multiple Intelligences

Activity	Verbal/Linguistic	Logical/Mathematical	Visual/Spatial	Musical/Rhythmic	Bodily/Kinesthetic	Naturalist	Interpersonal	Intrapersonal
Creating the Ensemble								
Finger Tip Trip	●		●		●		●	
Squishy Ball			●		●		●	
Sit Circle			●		●		●	
Creative Communication	●	●					●	
Arm Tangle	●	●			●		●	
Pass the Rope, Please!	●	●			●		●	
Body Machine	●	●		●	●		●	
Becoming a Storm				●	●		●	●
The Sounds & Smells of Memories				●			●	●
Movement Canon			●	●	●		●	
Pass the Ball to the Beat				●	●		●	
Mirror, Mirror			●	●	●		●	
Find Your Center					●		●	
Shoulder to Shoulder				●	●		●	
Song of the Day				●			●	●
Machine Soundscapes	●			●	●		●	
Huddle-Up	●		●		●		●	
Slap-It				●	●		●	
Bibbity Bop Bop Boo				●	●		●	
Language Arts								
A Line at a Time	●	●					●	
The ABC's of Storytelling	●						●	
Story Theater	●	●		●	●		●	
The Talk Back Talk Show	●				●		●	
Sounding Out Your Story	●	●		●			●	
Sound Effect Stories	●	●		●			●	
Character Monologues	●	●			●		●	
Readin', Rhymin', & Rhythm	●			●			●	
Recreating the Classics	●				●		●	●

The Dramatically Different Classroom • Christine Laitta & Mark Weakland
Kagan Publishing • 1 (800) WEE CO-OP • www.KaganOnline.com

Chart of Multiple Intelligences

Activity	Verbal/Linguistic	Logical/Mathematical	Visual/Spatial	Musical/Rhythmic	Bodily/Kinesthetic	Naturalist	Interpersonal	Intrapersonal
Language Arts Continued								
If They Were Alive Today	●	●		●	●		●	●
A Real Life Fairy Tale	●						●	●
Radio Theater	●	●		●			●	●
Music for Language Learning	●			●			●	●
A Picture Is Worth a Thousand Words	●	●			●		●	
The Missing Middle	●	●			●		●	
What's Your Sign?	●				●		●	
Poetry Soundscapes	●			●	●			
Feelings, Nothing More Than...	●			●	●		●	●
Tell Me a Story	●	●	●		●		●	●
Stories That Move Me	●		●		●		●	
The Story of My Life So Far	●		●	●	●		●	●
Express Yourself	●						●	●
Sing, Sing a Song	●			●			●	●
I Hear a Melody	●			●	●		●	●
Rhythm & Reading	●			●	●			
Elliptical Scenes	●	●	●		●		●	
History of Storytelling	●		●	●	●		●	●
Social Studies								
Little Schoolhouse on the Prairie	●		●				●	
The State I'm In	●	●	●		●		●	
Tableaux	●	●	●		●		●	
Step Inside a Painting	●		●		●		●	●
Wax Museum	●		●		●			
Talkin' History	●	●	●		●		●	●
Voices From the Past	●	●	●		●		●	●
The Flip Side: Seeing the Other Side of History	●	●	●		●		●	●
Our Town	●	●	●		●		●	●
Eating Goober Peas	●			●	●			●

Chart of Multiple Intelligences

Activity	Verbal/Linguistic	Logical/Mathematical	Visual/Spatial	Musical/Rhythmic	Bodily/Kinesthetic	Naturalist	Interpersonal	Intrapersonal
Social Studies Continued								
What If?	●	●					●	
Beginning, No Middle, the End	●	●					●	
The Oregon Trail Comes Alive	●	●	●		●		●	●
World Music	●			●				
Create a Culture	●		●	●	●		●	●
Family Tree	●		●		●		●	
The Republocratic Party	●	●	●				●	●
President for a Day	●	●	●				●	●
Through the Eye of a Lens	●		●				●	●
Mock Trials	●	●			●		●	●
The History of Art	●	●	●		●		●	●
Mathematics								
Alice's Restaurant	●	●			●		●	
Larger Than Life Math	●	●	●		●	●	●	
Vacation Stations	●	●			●		●	●
Scavenger Hunt	●	●	●		●	●	●	
Greatest Hits	●	●		●				
Math Theater	●	●			●		●	
Place Your Order	●	●					●	
The Math Shack	●	●	●		●		●	
How Many Borps in a Mile?	●	●	●		●		●	
Build It With Bodies	●	●			●		●	
Tower of London	●	●	●		●		●	
Movement Review		●	●		●		●	
All in the Family		●	●		●		●	
Building an Arch	●	●	●		●		●	●
Architecture That Works	●	●	●		●		●	●
Teacher for a Day	●	●	●	●	●		●	●
Architects: Making a Difference	●	●	●		●		●	●

The Dramatically Different Classroom • Christine Laitta & Mark Weakland
Kagan Publishing • 1 (800) WEE CO-OP • www.KaganOnline.com

Chart of Multiple Intelligences

Activity	Verbal/Linguistic	Logical/Mathematical	Visual/Spatial	Musical/Rhythmic	Bodily/Kinesthetic	Naturalist	Interpersonal	Intrapersonal
Science								
Soaring Through the Solar System	●	●	●		●	●	●	
Bunsen Burners & Other Hot Topics	●	●	●		●	●	●	
Let's Make It Move		●	●	●	●		●	
Journey to the Center of the Earth	●		●		●	●	●	
I Am a Tree	●		●		●	●	●	
Family Tree	●	●	●			●	●	●
It's Alive	●	●	●		●	●	●	
Songs of Science	●			●				●
Go With the Flow H$_2$O	●		●	●	●	●	●	
Conservation: Preserving a Place for the Future	●	●	●		●	●	●	
Only Skin Deep	●		●		●	●	●	
Digestion: The Inside Story	●		●	●	●	●	●	
Hygiene: The Whole Dirty Story	●		●		●	●	●	●
Diseases: Spreading the Truth	●		●		●	●	●	●
Safety Hero	●	●	●	●	●		●	
Building the Food Pyramid	●		●		●	●	●	●
Taking a Break								
Do a Little Dance				●	●			
Eraser Tag					●		●	
You Have Changed	●		●		●		●	
Lanterns			●		●			
Scavenger Hunt		●			●			
7-Up		●			●		●	
Who's the Leader?		●	●		●		●	
Who Am I?	●	●	●		●		●	
Improvisation With Specific Words	●	●	●		●		●	
Class TV			●		●		●	
Moving Music				●				
Bend & Stretch				●	●		●	
"Figure" It Out		●	●		●		●	

The Dramatically Different Classroom • Christine Laitta & Mark Weakland

Kagan Publishing • 1 (800) WEE CO-OP • www.KaganOnline.com

Acknowledgments

Dedicated to all the teachers who have inspired and nurtured us.

Special thanks to Elizabeth Good and Miguel Kagan for their support.

Christine wishes to personally thank Nancy Steen Laitta and Richard Laitta.

Mark wishes to personally thank Lynne Weakland and Elizabeth Good.

The creative book layout was designed by Denise Alphabet and Alex Core.
LaVonne Taylor edited the text.
Celso Rodriguez created the illustrations.
Miguel Kagan served as the consultant and project manager.

x

The Dramatically Different Classroom Christine Laitta & Mark Weakland
Kagan Publishing • 1 (800) WEE CO-OP • www.KaganOnline.com

Introduction
(What it is)

Rationale:
Find the Einstein, Hepburn, and Shakespeare Within!

• *We believe that teachers should use music, art and theater in their curriculum on a regular basis. Why? Because intelligence manifests itself in many ways!* In the 1980s Howard Gardner, a research scientist from Harvard University, put forth the idea of multiple intelligences. Drawing on various areas of brain and learning research, Dr. Gardner postulated a list of eight intelligences: linguistic, logical/mathematical, spatial, musical, bodily/kinesthetic, interpersonal, intra-personal and naturalist. *The Dramatically Different Classroom* is a book to help teachers recognize and nurture multiple intelligences in their students! Unlike activities and lessons that only teach to students with linguistic and logical/mathematical strengths, these activities speak to all students, especially those who learn through movement and music. *These activities reach out to students who have strengths in music and drama, love to move and make sounds, learn best when they can manipulate objects and are adept at working with others and understanding their own motivations and strengths.*

• *Music, art and drama are everywhere;* they do not exist solely as academic subjects in theater and music departments. Ask yourself this question on a daily basis: How can I integrate music and drama into my lesson? Look to movies, CDs, television, radio, plays, and videos as sources of ideas and inspiration. Remember that music teachers, your neighbor, a piano teacher, local artists, and many others can be great resources. Don't forget to draw on your own musical loves (from Nirvana to Perry Como) and your own talents (dust off that flute in the closet and break out the easel).

• **The Dramatically Different Classroom** *celebrates the diversity of students' intelligences and abilities with activities that promote an inclusive classroom environment.* Two goals of this book are: 1) helping classroom teachers adapt to and program for the individual educational needs of all students, and 2) making information tangible and living to the students (turning abstract concepts into concrete examples). Classroom teachers are called upon to reach out and teach to all students, regardless of present achievement levels or over-all ability. Classrooms now contain students who use English as a second language, need learning support and come from amazingly diverse cultural backgrounds. Inclusive classrooms contain students who have nontraditional learning styles or need to learn how to cooperate and concentrate. The activities in this book help teachers meet the needs of all students and provide them with a wide variety of learning opportunities. In other words, *The Dramatically Different Classroom* provides students with new ways to learn the same old stuff!

The Dramatically Different Classroom • Christine Laitta & Mark Weakland
Kagan Publishing • 1 (800) WEE CO-OP • www.KaganOnline.com

xi

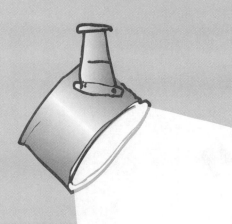

• *Music and drama encourage teachers and students to think outside of the box and dare to be different.* They reconnect teachers to a creative side (that may have been tucked away in a drawer with the whiteout and rubber bands) while creating in students a desire to take risks and try new ideas. The theory of multiple intelligences says that intelligence is not static; neither is one's ability to learn. When properly nurtured and stimulated, the intelligences of an individual are activated and developed by the activity in which he or she participates. Therefore, the activities in this book have been designed to nurture and stimulate all types of intelligences and promote growth and development in as many educational areas as possible. Instead of simply writing or reading to learn, students create living pictures, compose soundscapes, study in their communities and the natural environment, bring inanimate objects to life, dress and act as if they lived in another century and work in cooperative groups that build science machines with their bodies and soar through the solar system!

• *Music and drama are often used to enhance a lesson, but in the minds of the students they are the lesson!* For example, when a teacher adds to her lesson by singing the times tables, she may think she was simply doing something extra special. Actually, singing is the activity that solidifies the lesson's content in the minds of the students. *If music and drama are so memorable to students, why not use them to teach the whole lesson?*

• Take a minute and think back to the most interesting and inspiring moments that you experienced when you were a student. Do they include field trips, assemblies, and class plays? Weren't the best times when you shared something you made, took part in a group activity like Classroom Olympics, or did something special such as reading to the second graders. *These memorable moments can happen every day if you rethink your lessons in terms of music and drama.*

• When teachers use creative dramatic techniques and music early in the school year and use them consistently, *students develop natural interactions between one another and become comfortable with nonthreatening physical expression and contact.* An early start and regular usage of this book's activities will hook the students on movement, music, and drama. Soon your students will want to create their own activities and will expect other teachers to use drama and music, too.

• *The ensemble activities in this book, as well as many of the academic activities, are designed to foster acceptance of others, create trust and cooperation among students, and encourage positive risk taking.* The Dramatically Different Classroom provides teachers with activities that allow students to become comfortable with peers and adults and accept, and even celebrate, the differences of others. Under stress from difficult home lives, impoverished neighborhoods and a

xii

The Dramatically Different Classroom • Christine Laitta & Mark Weakland
Kagan Publishing • 1 (800) WEE CO-OP • www.KaganOnline.com

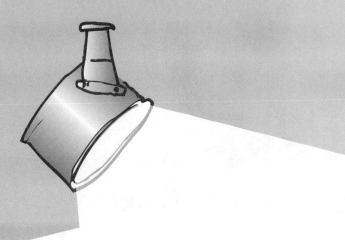

lack of a social supports many students come to school without the prerequisite skills needed for learning. If students are worried about being teased by others, arc ultracompetitive or feel alone and misunderstood, they cannot be ready to concentrate on binomial equations and prepositional phrases! And so teachers must take steps to teach students how to cooperate, take risks, become less competitive, and form a circle of supportive friends. Whether one calls a group of students a cooperative learning group, a classroom community or an ensemble, the focus of this book remains the same: it aims to provide teachers with activities that promote peaceful and respectful co-existence in the classroom.

• *Current research tells us that music and movement are important, some would say vital, in the overall education of any child.* Articles in *Newsweek* and other national magazines have described how music is linked to mathematical thinking. Brain research has shown that physical skills and emotional responses increase the strength of memory pathways and improve the chance that learning will "stick." A lesson that has an emotional impact is more likely to be remembered than a lesson that is interesting but doesn't illicit an emotional response. Research also tells us that some people are right-brain dominant while others are left-brain dominant. Students with right-brain dominance learn best when presented with lessons and activities that emphasize music, emotions, and gross motor movement and de-emphasize words, numbers, and fine motor

movements. Some of the many factors that inhibit learning, such as competition, environmental stress, emotional stress, and lack of movement have now been systematically studied and identified. How does a teacher increase the emotional impact of a lesson and teach to students with right-brain dominance? *How can a teacher incorporate more music and movement into the busy school day and decrease competition and stress in the classroom? The answers to those questions are right here in this book!*

• *Oh yeah—music and drama are fun!*

The Dramatically Different Classroom • Christine Laitta & Mark Weakland
Kagan Publishing • 1 (800) WEE CO-OP • www.KaganOnline.com

xiii

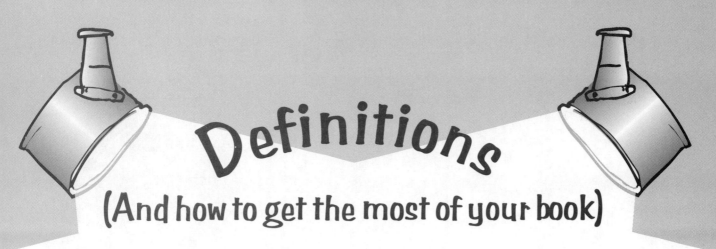

Definitions
(And how to get the most of your book)

• **An ensemble is a group of people working together to achieve a common goal.** If you are new to using creative dramatics and music in your lessons, the ensemble activities will help guide you through the process. **Ensemble activities are the building blocks for future lessons—try them first.**

• **Enhancers are ideas for moving the lesson up and down grade levels and/or enriching the curriculum.** Before you begin, read through the entire lesson, especially the enhancers. Reading the enhancers may spark an idea on how to tailor the lesson to your specific class or to individual students.

• **Side coaching is a series of gentle reminders from the teacher during the course of the activity.** By reminding the students (with a soft vocal quality) of what they need to do or say, the teacher keeps the lessons on track and moving forward. For examples of side coaching, see Story Theater (Activity 3 in the Language Arts section) and Becoming a Storm (Activity 8 in the Ensemble section).

• **Many activities have explicit or implicit classroom management strategies built right into them. These built-in rules and regulations allow your class to do creative dramatics.** For example, the teacher may use the peace sign for a lesson and may say "when the peace sign is shown, it means peace and quiet (and all eyes and ears focused on the teacher)." These management strategies, sometimes created by the students, give them a sense of ownership, provide them with a chance to do the activities they enjoy, and motivate them to monitor and discipline each other in a positive way. Although they may change from lesson to lesson, they always help the teacher maintain structure in the classroom. Before getting the students up on their feet and engaged, remind them of the expectations and the objectives of the lesson.

• **Roleplaying and reenactment are encouraged. The students are expected to get up on their feet, add movement and sounds to lessons, take on the roles of characters, and perform monologues and skits.** As you begin the lesson, keep an open mind, a sense of adventure and a willingness to take chances. Don't be afraid to suggest interracial and transgender casting! If the teacher is willing to experiment, the students will be inspired to do the same.

The Dramatically Different Classroom • Christine Laitta & Mark Weakland
Kagan Publishing • 1 (800) WEE CO-OP • www.KaganOnline.com

xiv

- **Take time to troubleshoot the activity before you launch into it.** Consider physical issues that your students may have, their age and maturity level, and their need for personal space. At the same time, be willing to be in the moment and address issues as they come up. For example, while preparing to do the Sit Circle (Activity 3 in the Ensemble section, page 4), a child may comment on another's size ("Hey, he'll break my lap!"). Be willing to step into the circle and teach by example.

- **Write notes to yourself in the margins of the lesson.** Describe what worked best for you and what you changed or modified to make the lesson work. If you come up with an idea that suits your class, jot it down. Then share your ideas with fellow teachers.

- **Use stage directions when rehearsing dramatic classroom activities.** The terms "stage right," "stage left," "upstage" and "downstage" are used in professional theater. You may want to use these terms when utilizing space during activities such as Wax Museum (page 85), Our Town (page 90), or many of the Ensemble activities. Try using these terms when staging your school play. See the floor plan of the stage (page xvii) for more details.

Other ways to get the most out of your book:
- It makes a great gift
- Use it to even out a wobbly table
- Use it as a coaster
- It makes a great gift
- Press your fall leaves in it
- On hot days, fan yourself with it
- It makes a great gift

The Dramatically Different Classroom • Christine Laitta & Mark Weakland
Kagan Publishing • 1 (800) WEE CO-OP • www.KaganOnline.com

XV

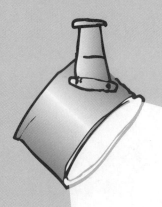

Preview
(What you're gonna get)

- Making the abstract concrete is what this book is all about. It is chock full of ideas for changing the physical setting of your classroom, expressing facts, concepts and ideas through movement, drama and music, and making thoughts and concepts tangible and real.

- You don't need to do mounds of paperwork to bring music and drama into lessons. We've done it for you!

- This book is organized into eight chapters which contain activities for teaching everything from social studies to math. The first chapter, full of activities for building a classroom ensemble, contains the building blocks for the rest of the book.

- Each activity is set up in the following manner:
  - A description of the objectives.
  - A list of materials that you will need.
  - Background information that you need to know before you begin.
  - Step-by-step instructions on teaching the activity.
  - Enhancers that give ideas for adapting the activity to your students' grade/ability level.
  - The multiple intelligences that the activity speaks to.

The Dramatically Different Classroom • Christine Laitta & Mark Weakland
Kagan Publishing • 1 (800) WEE CO-OP • www.KaganOnline.com

Stage Floor Plan

Upstage Right (UR)	**Upstage Center (UC)**	**Upstage Left (UL)**
Stage Right (SR)	**Center Stage (CS)**	**Stage Left (SL)**
Downstage Right (DSR)	**Downstage Center (DSC)**	**Downstage Left (DSL)**

W I N G S (left)   W I N G S (right)

Audience   Audience   Audience

*The directions are always given from the actor's perspective (facing the audience).

The Dramatically Different Classroom • Christine Laitta & Mark Weakland
Kagan Publishing • 1 (800) WEE CO-OP • www.KaganOnline.com

xvii

Creating the Ensemble

(Setting the Stage)

Activities that help students work together

The Dramatically Different Classroom • Christine Laitta & Mark Weakland
Kagan Publishing • 1 (800) WEE CO-OP • www.KaganOnline.com

1

Finger Tip Trip

As a sighted student guides a blindfolded student by the tips of his or her fingers, students create trust among one another and rediscover their senses.

Stuff You Need

• Blindfolds
• Interesting objects

Stuff You Need to Know

This can be done in the classroom or outside in an open area.

Enhancers

• Have the students try to build a huge tower of blocks with a blindfolded partner or allow them to create their own tasks, such as tying shoes, getting dressed or making a cookie recipe. The sighted partner should physically and verbally assist as needed.
• Now let them try to build a tower using verbal coaching and no physical help.

Multiple Intelligences

• Visual/Spatial
• Bodily/Kinesthetic
• Interpersonal
• Verbal/Linguistic

1. Partner Up

Partner up each student. Remind the partners that one person will be the eyes for the other.

2. The Sighted Guide the Blind

The sighted student guides the blindfolded student around the room or playground, successfully navigating around obstacles.

3. Blind Discover Objects

The sighted student guides the blindfolded student by the tips of her/his fingers to several different objects. Once there, the blindfolded student feels the objects and describes what they feel like in as much detail as possible.

4. Return to Start

The sighted student brings his partner back to the spot where he started and removes the blindfold. Now the previously "blind" person tries to find the objects that he touched earlier.

5. Switch Roles

Switch partners and do the same activity.

The Dramatically Different Classroom • Christine Laitta & Mark Weakland
Kagan Publishing • 1 (800) WEE CO-OP • www.KaganOnline.com

Squishy Ball

Students pass a squishy ball around in a circle using only their elbows or knees. Hands may not be used and the students cannot drop the ball in this timed event. This is a great "get to know your classmates" activity as well as one that promotes bonding within a group.

Stuff You Need

- One nerf-type, squishy ball that is at least as large as a soccer ball
- A clear space in which to form a circle

1. Form a Circle

Students form a circle in which everyone is facing the middle. One person places the ball between his or her knees. Remind the class that you will be timing them.

2. Pass the Ball

The students pass the ball to each other around the circle using only their knees. If they drop it, they start over!

3. Time the Group

Time the group. After they successfully pass the ball all the way around, go back and do it again in half the time!

Stuff You Need to Know

The teacher leads the activity by timing the event. Remind the class that they will become a stronger and faster team if they encourage each other. If they drop the ball, they must start again.

Enhancers

- Pass the squishy ball with elbows instead of knees or start with the elbows and then move to the knees.
- Chart the progress of your class on the board and compare it to the progress of others. Have the students construct their own graphs during a math class.

Multiple Intelligences

- Visual/Spatial
- Bodily/Kinesthetic
- Interpersonal

The Dramatically Different Classroom • Christine Laitta & Mark Weakland
Kagan Publishing • 1 (800) WEE CO-OP • www.KaganOnline.com

3

Sit Circle

By sitting on the lap of the person behind them, the students build a human circle that supports itself. This activity builds trust among students.

Stuff You Need

• A large, clear space

Stuff You Need to Know

This is a quick activity that can be done with a classroom of students or even an entire school. Remind the students that people need to support one another every day.

Multiple Intelligences

• Visual/Spatial
• Bodily/Kinesthetic
• Interpersonal

1. Form a Circle

Form your group into a circle where everyone is facing the same way.

2. Work Together

On the count of three, everyone sits down slowly on the lap of the person behind them. The group supports itself! It really works!

3. Stand Up Together

On the count of three, stand up carefully!

The Dramatically Different Classroom • Christine Laitta & Mark Weakland
Kagan Publishing • 1 (800) WEE CO-OP • www.KaganOnline.com

Creative Communication

Students create an imaginary vocabulary and teach it to one another. This activity introduces the concept of a foreign language and promotes creative problem solving.

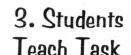

1. Choose a Challenge

Have each child pick a task he or she would like to teach to the class.

2. Prepare the Vocabulary

Let the students prepare a vocabulary based on words needed to teach the task. They need to write down this vocabulary and the meaning of their words. As you start, give the students examples of simple tasks, such as buttoning a coat, brushing your hair or shaking hands.

See examples in the following blackline master.

3. Students Teach Task

Have the student or students teach the task to the class. (Say that five times fast!)

4. Discuss and Critique

Discuss what the class learned from the presentation. Was it easy to follow, did they use movements that complemented their words, what else could the students have used to make their presentation more clear?

Stuff You Need

- Examples of a created vocabulary complete with a meaning for each word
- Paper and pencil
- Imaginary Words blackline master

Stuff You Need to Know

Students can do this activity with a partner, in cooperative groups or as a whole class. Make sure they have plenty of time to prepare. Remind them that the created vocabulary must be large enough to teach the task. In this activity, students learn that people with disabilities or those who don't speak English must overcome language and communication barriers every day.

Enhancers

- Substitute other challenges, such as No Sight or No Hands (see Activity 1, Finger Tip Trip, page 2).
- Discuss other challenges that make learning and communicating difficult, such as traveling to a foreign country or communicating with someone who has a hearing impairment.
- Create your own vocabulary. Use these made up words to encourage and praise the students.

Multiple Intelligences

- Interpersonal
- Verbal/Linguistic
- Logical/Mathematical

The Dramatically Different Classroom • Christine Laitta & Mark Weakland
Kagan Publishing • 1 (800) WEE CO-OP • www.KaganOnline.com

5

gangtuup: stand up
jeezee = good
yanno = no

Imaginary Words

Name_____ Date_____

A. Here are some examples of
imaginary words and their meanings

1. gang tuup   =   stand up
2. jeez   =   good!
3. yanno   =   no
4. huup so   =   down

B. Here are a few more imaginary words. You write down what they mean.

1. grib meen   = _____

2. borp   = _____

3. wiggy   = _____

4. huhza   = _____

5. cheeble flex = _____

C. In the following seven spaces, write down seven imaginary words.
Then write their meanings.

1. _____ = _____

2. _____ = _____

3. _____ = _____

4. _____ = _____

5. _____ = _____

6. _____ = _____

7. _____ = _____

The Dramatically Different Classroom • Christine Laitta & Mark Weakland
Kagan Publishing • 1 (800) WEE CO-OP • www.KaganOnline.com

Arm Tangle

After forming a large and tangled group, students must untangle their arms and reform a circle without letting go of anyone's hands. This activity points out potential classroom leaders to the teacher. Students learn to compromise, listen, and problem solve. In addition to teamwork and trust, spatial reasoning and the ability to see spatial relationships are also promoted.

1. Discuss Ensemble

Redefine "ensemble" for the class and give everyday life examples, such as firefighters working together to put out a blaze.

2. Give a Hand

Students form small groups of five to six students. As the students stand and face one another in a circle, each one reaches across and takes the hand of two different people.

3. Students Work Together to Get Free

Give the command, "Untangle yourself without letting go!" Remind the students to think as an ensemble.

4. The Circle Game

The end result should be one large circle or two smaller interlocking ones. Just so you know, students may end up facing the opposite direction.

Stuff You Need

• A clear space

Stuff You Need to Know

This can be done in small or large groups. The larger the group, the more difficult it is. Remind the students that no one should ever be in danger of getting hurt and they must work together to prevent this! If they "mess up," they must start again.

Enhancers

• This is a good activity for teachers, too!
• Increase the number of students in the circle until the whole class is working together.

Multiple Intelligences

• Interpersonal
• Logical/Mathematical
• Verbal/Linguistic
• Bodily/Kinesthetic

The Dramatically Different Classroom • Christine Laitta & Mark Weakland
Kagan Publishing • 1 (800) WEE CO-OP • www.KaganOnline.com

7

Pass the Rope, Please!

Standing in a circle and holding hands, students perform acts of physical contortion in order to pass along a circle of rope without letting go of each others' hands. Students verbally communicate with one another in order to accomplish the task.

Stuff You Need

• A clear space
• A piece of clothesline approximately six feet long tied into a circle. The smaller the kids, the smaller the circle of rope!

Stuff You Need to Know

This can be done in small or large groups. The larger the group, the more difficult it is and the longer it will take to pass the rope. Depending upon how the rope is positioned in relationship to the child's body, it may be easier or more difficult to pass the rope. Imagine that the rope is traveling clockwise. The rope is between the wrists of two students. To pass it clockwise, the student has to wiggle it down her arm and up to her shoulder. This is the easy part. Now, without letting go and without the direct use of her hands, the student has to maneuver it around her head, under her underarm and down her body to the floor. It sounds crazy, but it works!

Multiple Intelligences

• Interpersonal
• Logical/Mathematical
• Verbal/Lingusitc
• Bodily/Kinesthetic

1. Form a Circle

Have the students stand in a circle and show them the circle of rope.

2. Hang a Rope

Choose one student as the starting point. Hang the circle of rope around that student's wrist, then have the entire group join hands.

3. Figure It Out

Present the problem: with connected hands, how can we pass this rope around the circle? The students are free to move their bodies and help each other in any way they can, but they cannot let go of each other's hands.

The Dramatically Different Classroom • Christine Laitta & Mark Weakland
Kagan Publishing • 1 (800) WEE CO-OP • www.KaganOnline.com

Body Machine

Using movements and sounds, students develop a human machine. The machine can be one that you are currently studying, for example a steel mill or a cotton gin or something crazy and original that the students create, like a bubble gum factory. Students learn creative problem solving, spatial relations, and how to work as an ensemble.

1. Discuss Machines

Discuss how objects are made with assembly lines, machines and robots. Pick an object that is made by a machine and discuss what steps are needed to produce the product.

2. Pick a Project

Decide on what the class wants to make. The teacher should demonstrate how movement and sound go together. For example, if you need a cutter in your machine, you can swing your arms back and forth and make a sound like air being pushed (fff..tt, fff..tt) and materials being cut (shhwhit, shhwit).

3. Create It

Ask the students to create movements and sounds that are specific to what is being made. Give them time to experiment.

4. Bring It to Life

Now start building. Begin with someone doing a movement and a sound. Ask them what their specific job is in the machine. How will it effect the final creation? After the student answers, place this student in the front of the classroom and ask others "How can we add to the machine?"

5. Plug 'Em In

Add each student until the entire group is making the final product. The students must interrelate and work together.

6. Team Machines

Using the Machine Blueprint blackline, teams build a body machine and share it with the class.

Stuff You Need

- A clear space big enough for the whole class
- Machine Blueprint blackline master

Stuff You Need to Know

Before you begin this activity, make sure your students have an understanding of how the parts of machines and assembly lines work together. The manager is the teacher because he or she will choose students one at a time and add him or her to the machine. Consider the teacher to be the "foreman." An additional management strategy could be a whistle to stop the action. Add each student after you have asked "What does your sound and movement represent? How does it add to the final product?"

Enhancers

- Speed it up, slow it down.
- Build another one.
- Discuss: how could the machine become more efficient?
- Use Tinker Toys or Legos and blocks as an extension of your body.

Multiple Intelligences

- Interpersonal
- Logical/Mathematical
- Verbal/Linguistic
- Bodily/Kinesthetic
- Musical/Rhythmic

The Dramatically Different Classroom • Christine Laitta & Mark Weakland
Kagan Publishing • 1 (800) WEE CO-OP • www.KaganOnline.com

9

Machine Blueprint

As a team, select a machine to build. Each person will be a part of the machine. Fill out the movement, sound and function for each part below, then draw a picture of the machine.

Movement	Sound	Function
1. _____	_____	_____
2. _____	_____	_____
3. _____	_____	_____
4. _____	_____	_____
5. _____	_____	_____
6. _____	_____	_____

Draw a picture of the body machine!

The Dramatically Different Classroom • Christine Laitta & Mark Weakland
Kagan Publishing • 1 (800) WEE CO-OP • www.KaganOnline.com

Becoming a Storm

Students tell the story of a rainstorm by using body sounds while the teacher side coaches them in order to keep the story moving. Students work as an ensemble, learn the sequence of a storm, and how to follow directions.

1. A Drizzle Begins

Sit in a circle on the floor
- Snap your fingers. Say, "this is the pitter patter of tiny raindrops. A rainstorm is approaching!"

2. Raindrops Keep Fallin' on My Head

The following movements and side coachings are suggestions for simulating the crescendo of the rainstorm:
- Slap your thighs while saying, "This is the beginning of the downpour."
- Slap the floor while saying, "That must be the rain hitting the tin roof."
- Stomp your feet on the floor and say, "Those must be the people running for cover."

3. Storm Ends

Now reverse the order until it is just the students snapping their fingers. This is the storm ending.

4. Life in a Storm

Take this activity a step further by having one group continue to be the storm while another group becomes a forest with animals, birds, flowers and trees. How do they react?

Stuff You Need

- A clear space

Stuff You Need to Know

Stomping on the floor creates the sound of thunder and heavy rain. Each body movement is a part of the rainstorm. The teacher side coaches (with a soft vocal quality) and the students must listen for their cues. Remind the students that people learn a great deal by listening! During any given movement and sound, direct the students to increase the volume (crescendo—your new vocabulary word!) or decrease the volume (decrescendo).

Enhancers

- Create your own sounds for rain.
- Discuss how sounds alone can tell a story. What other stories can be told with just sounds?
- Try creating another story with just sounds. The teacher can model an example and then the class can try one of their own.

Multiple Intelligences

- Interpersonal
- Bodily/Kinesthetic
- Musical/Rhythmic
- Intrapersonal

The Dramatically Different Classroom • Christine Laitta & Mark Weakland
Kagan Publishing • 1 (800) WEE CO-OP • www.KaganOnline.com

11

The Sounds & Smells of Memories

Students brainstorm sounds and smells that trigger strong memories. They share these sounds and smells with others and then share the images and memories that are associated with each smell and sound. Sharing sounds and smells builds ensemble by allowing students to share personal thoughts and memories with one another.

Stuff You Need

• Recording equipment, such as a tape recorder.

Stuff You Need to Know

This activity activates senses and neural pathways that may not be engaged during an average school day. Pairing images with the senses of hearing and smell strengthens memories. Although smells in school can be problematic and sometimes unpleasant, enjoyable and pleasant smells are a very important part of emotions and memories. Some research has shown that smells may help form memories that are stronger and longer-lasting than others.

1. Discuss Sound and Memories

Discuss how sounds can trigger memories of past events. Give a personal example of how a sound triggered a memory in you. Ask the question, "When memories are triggered by sounds, what actions can result?" Brainstorm a short list of sounds that trigger memories of families and friends. Then place the students in small groups and have them brainstorm a longer list of memory-triggering sounds.

2. Bringing in the Sounds

Have students gather sounds, not only from their own experiences, such as playground noises, a sound bite from a favorite TV show or their mothers calling them, but also sounds from family experiences, such as the sound of ocean waves from a vacation or the sounds of a diner (grill sizzling and cars honking). The students may bring in the sound if it is made by a small object (such as an alarm clock or a music box) or record it using a tape recorder.

3. Share the Sounds

Put the students in small groups of three or four and have them share and discuss their sounds.

The Dramatically Different Classroom • Christine Laitta & Mark Weakland
Kagan Publishing • 1 (800) WEE CO-OP • www.KaganOnline.com

4. Create a Sound Library

Find time to record and catalog each student's sounds and memories. You may want to delegate this activity to an especially motivated and responsible group of students. By the end of the activity, each student should have a library of sounds and stories that preserve a piece of their history.

5. Get Ready for a Smelly Party

Broaden the scope of this activity by including smells that trigger memories. With the students, brainstorm a short list of smells, such as bread baking, the smell of a swimming pool's chlorine or seaweed, that trigger memories of families and friends. Then place the students in small groups and have them brainstorm a longer list of memory-triggering smells.

6. Throw a Smelly Party

Have your students bring in materials that have a strong and unique smell to them. These materials, such as Grandma's perfume, a gingerbread cookie or Dad's cologne should produce odors that remind the students of particular people or situations. If possible, put the odoriferous material in a small plastic cup or spray it on a card. Model how to gently hold the material under a peer's nose (you may have to reinforce how to do this appropriately) and encourage the other to take a "whiff." Have the students share the smells and talk about what memories the smells trigger.

Enhancers

- Include the sound audiotape in a student's portfolio.
- Collect all the students' sounds and memories and make a listening and learning center.

Multiple Intelligences

- Interpersonal
- Intrapersonal
- Musical/Rhythmic

The Dramatically Different Classroom • Christine Laitta & Mark Weakland
Kagan Publishing • 1 (800) WEE CO-OP • www.KaganOnline.com

13

Movement Canon

The students memorize a specific movement that the teacher makes and then replicate it, while at the same time learning a new movement. Use this activity to increase music reading skills and focus attention. In this activity, students must think ahead in order to move simultaneously with others.

Stuff You Need

• A clear space for students to move in

Stuff You Need to Know

A canon is a composition, usually employing the voice, that uses imitation. Share this definition with the students so they don't think you are talking about artillery! Your students should know how to keep the beat and should be able to do large motor movements. You can adapt this activity for all age levels (see Enhancers).

Enhancers

• Have a student lead the class.
• Try harder or "crazier" movements for older kids.
• Teacher and students sit in a circle. The teacher starts a movement. The student to her immediate left picks up the movement after four beats. The teacher begins a new movement. The students "pass" each new movement to the person sitting next to them. Eventually, the "old" movement will return to the teacher and the canon stops.
• Instead of a physical canon, try a vocal canon. In this activity, the teacher would say a word four times in a row. The students repeat this word four times while the teacher speaks a new word.

Multiple Intelligences

• Interpersonal
• Musical/Rhythmic
• Bodily/Kinesthetic
• Visual/Spatial

1. We've Got the Beat

Start with a "keep the beat" warm-up. This simply involves clapping out quarter notes or one, two, three, four. As you clap, have the students keep the beat with you.

2. Pete and Repeat

The teacher says, "I'm going to do a movement and I want you to repeat it when I am done. While you are doing that movement, I am going to start another one." Remember that after the teacher completes the first movement, two movements will be going on simultaneously!

Example:
Teacher: claps hands four times
Students: watch the teacher
Teacher: taps her head four times
Students: clap hands four times
Teacher: snaps fingers four times
Students: tap heads four times

3. Do It Again and Again

Continue until the students have mastered this skill.

The Dramatically Different Classroom • Christine Laitta & Mark Weakland
Kagan Publishing • 1 (800) WEE CO-OP • www.KaganOnline.com

Pass the Ball to the Beat

The group passes a ball around a circle to the beat of a song. This activity is great for increasing attention, concentration, listening, and motor ability. It also develops rhythmic awareness and teamwork.

1. Keep the Beat

Sit in a circle and practice clapping together to keep the beat. Practice clapping faster and slower. The teacher sets the tempo and everyone must stay together.

2. Pass It

Pass a ball around the circle to the beat.

Stuff You Need

- Small, soft ball or bean bag
- Tape recorder and music with a pronounced beat
- A large, clear space

Stuff You Need to Know

The beat is the control device as is the teacher's ability to stop the music. Creating or choosing music with a strong beat will keep the students focused. You can keep the beat by simply hitting two sticks together, using a small drum or having the class sing a song. As the children become more accomplished, pick some fun music for ball or bean bag passing and make sure it has a strong beat. The Beatles' *Birthday* is a good example of a song with a strong beat. You can also use *We Will Rock You* by Queen or John Philip Sousa's *Stars and Stripes Forever*.
See R.M. Abramson in the bibliography for more on rhythm games and activities.

Enhancers

- Pass the ball to faster and faster music.
- Sing while you pass the ball.
- To promote listening, stop the music and see if the students are able to freeze when the music stops. Also, call out "reverse!" When this happens, the students must reverse directions.

Multiple Intelligences

- Interpersonal
- Musical/Rhythmic
- Bodily/Kinesthetic

The Dramatically Different Classroom • Christine Laitta & Mark Weakland
Kagan Publishing • 1 (800) WEE CO-OP • www.KaganOnline.com

Mirror, Mirror

As they stand face to face with a partner and maintain eye contact, students duplicate the movements of their partner. This is a focusing and movement activity that helps children relate to one another and move as a single unit.

Stuff You Need

• A space big enough to have everyone standing face to face with their partner.

Stuff You Need to Know

This focused activity requires two people to move in unison, perfectly mirroring one another. The person who is leading should be reminded that the slower they move, the easier it will be for the "mirror" to follow.

Enhancers

• Speed up the movements. Make the movements more subtle.
• Just do facial movements.
• Add classical music or other types of music that might create a particular movement mood such as happy, sad and angry.
• Try adding identical props.

Multiple Intelligences

• Interpersonal
• Bodily/Kinesthetic
• Musical/Rhythmic
• Visual/Spatial

1. Pair 'Em Up

Pair up each student. Stand them face to face.

2. Mirror, Mirror

Let them decide who will be the "mirror." The other person will be the leader. Explain that they must maintain eye contact at all times and they may have to use peripheral vision to continue the flow of movements.

3. Moooove Slooowly

Begin slow movements. Larger motor movements, such as bending from the waist or swinging arms, work best at the beginning stages.

4. Move Quickly

Try faster and smaller movements.

5. Switch

Switch leaders.

6. Reflections

Have the students reflect on what they have learned. What makes a good leader? What qualities are necessary to be a good mirror? (The authors prefer a large oak frame with antique beveled glass!) What was easy about the activity? What was hard?

The Dramatically Different Classroom • Christine Laitta & Mark Weakland
Kagan Publishing • 1 (800) WEE CO-OP • www.KaganOnline.com

Find Your Center

Students create a circle around a blindfolded person. The group, with their hands at chest level, keep the person standing by gently pushing him back to his center. This activity promotes trust and teamwork among classmates.

1. Choose the Middle Man

Choose a person to be in the middle. Put a blindfold on him and cross his arms over his chest. Others surround this person in a tight circle, standing shoulder to shoulder, arms at chest level.

2. Lean On Me

Tell the person in the middle to fall forward or backward with legs locked. As the blindfolded person does this, the others restore him or her to center.

3. Switch

Switch person in the middle.

Stuff You Need

- One blindfold
- A space to form circles

Stuff You Need to Know

Everyone is involved in keeping the middle person standing. The person in the middle will cross his arms on his chest and lock his legs. Other classmates surrounding this person in a tight circle, their hands at chest level, ready to gently push the man in the middle back to his center.

Enhancers

- Put on some music and try falling and restoring to the beat. Music suggestions: Prince's *Trust* or James Taylor's *You've Got a Friend.*

Multiple Intelligences

- Interpersonal
- Bodily/Kinesthetic

The Dramatically Different Classroom • Christine Laitta & Mark Weakland
Kagan Publishing • 1 (800) WEE CO-OP • www.KaganOnline.com

17

Shoulder to Shoulder

Standing in a large circle with one person in the middle, students connect body parts (such as elbow to elbow) as they keep the beat and rhythmically call out "student to student." The student in the middle directs the activity until "center to circle" is called out, at which time new pairs form, the circle regroups and a new student enters the middle to be "it." As the activity continues, students get to know one another and practice taking risks.

Stuff You Need

- A space large enough to form a circle

Stuff You Need to Know

Before engaging in this activity, students should be comfortable with physical contact and working in pairs. In the beginning, the teacher may allow the students to form their own pairs. The response "student to student" is an affirmation to the teacher that the students are indeed connected.

1. Pair Up

Before students form a circle, the teacher should group them in pairs. Everybody needs a partner. If there is an odd number, one student can join the teacher in the middle for the first round.

2. Circle Round

Students stand side-by-side with their paired partner and form a circle around the teacher. The center person, in this case the teacher, never has a partner.

3. Connect the Parts to the Beat

The person in the middle establishes a rhythm of steady fours by clapping or snapping his or her fingers. If they like, students can join in by snapping their fingers. Once everyone is keeping the beat, the person who is "it" calls out two body parts to the beat, such as "shoulder to shoulder" or "hand to back." The student pairs touch these parts and respond by saying in rhythm "student to student." Remember to keep the rhythm going and remember the pairs always stay in the circle. On the next set of beats, the students disconnect as "it" calls out a new set of body parts, such as "foot to foot" or "pinky to forehead." The students touch and say "student to student" in rhythm.

The Dramatically Different Classroom • Christine Laitta & Mark Weakland
Kagan Publishing • 1 (800) WEE CO-OP • www.KaganOnline.com

4. Regroup With a New "It"

The pairs continue to touch, say "student to student" and disconnect until the person in the middle calls out "center to circle." This is the cue for the center person to join the circle and all of the pairs to break up and find new partners. After a certain amount of scrambling, one person will be without a partner. This person is now the new "it" in the center.

5. Class Discussion

At some point the teacher should guide the class as they discuss the following questions:
* *What feelings did you have as you did this activity?*
* *Did you have to take some risks in this activity?*
* *What were they?*
* *Was it difficult or easy to pair up with a new partner?*

Enhancers

* Speed up the activity as students get better at working together and keeping the beat.
* Play a couple of rounds in which the students don't disconnect after each direction. They stay glued together (elbow to elbow, foot to foot) much like a game of "Twister" until "center to circle" is called out.
* Add music.

Multiple Intelligences

* Interpersonal
* Bodily/Kinesthetic
* Musical/Rhythmic

*Note: This activity is based on an idea from Ambrose Panico's **Classroom Community***

The Dramatically Different Classroom • Christine Laitta & Mark Weakland
Kagan Publishing • 1 (800) WEE CO-OP • www.KaganOnline.com

19

Song of the Day

After collecting a favorite song from each student, song titles are written on slips of paper. At the end of the day or during a special break time, the teacher randomly draws one slip of paper and plays that song for the class. As each student shares his or her song with the class, the teacher and classmates become better acquainted with that student and get turned onto some new and exciting music.

Stuff You Need

- Submitted songs from students on CD, tape or album (one from each student)
- A CD player, tape deck and/or record player
- Some of your own favorite songs to share
- Slips of paper (one for each song)
- Hat, box or bag to draw slips from

Stuff You Need to Know

Sharing music is an enriching and meaningful way to reward students or take a break in a hectic day. For students in middle and high school, music is an emotional outlet that often expresses feelings difficult to put into words. Knowing what music students are listening to can help the teacher to know them better. Music used for song of the day does not have to be a song. It can be part of a symphony or wordless musical piece. Students should be told up front that the teacher will review and approve all submitted songs before they are put into the box for the drawing.

1. Pick a Time, State the Purpose

The teacher decides when the Song of the Day will occur. It can start the day, end the day or provide for a break in the day. The teacher should also consider the purpose of the activity. Is it simply for fun, will additional verbal sharing and discussion go on and will the students be included unconditionally or will they have to earn the privilege of submitting a song?

2. Share a Song

The teacher shares two favorite songs or pieces of music with the class and talks about why he or she has picked this song to share. Topics for discussion can include comments about the words or instrumentation, special memories attached to the song and how it makes the teacher feel (sad, energized, wild, calm).

20

The Dramatically Different Classroom • Christine Laitta & Mark Weakland
Kagan Publishing • 1 (800) WEE CO-OP • www.KaganOnline.com

3. Students Submit a Song

Each student should submit one song to the teacher. After listening to each song, the teacher approves it or has the student pick a more appropriate piece.

4. Create Chance Coupons

Put each song title on a separate piece of paper, coupon or ticket. Then place them in a special box, bag, hat or jar.

5. Draw a Slip, Play a Song

At the decided time, the teacher pulls out one of the slips and that song is played! If desired, discussion can occur prior to the song or after the song. Consider letting the person whose song was picked draw out the next slip of paper.

6. Create a Master List and Start Again

After each student has taken a turn and all of the songs have been played, create a master list of student names and songs. Then start all over again!

Enhancers

• Take the concept to the principal and see if the entire school can join in the fun. Submitted songs can be played over the intercom at the beginning or end of the day.

Multiple Intelligences

• Interpersonal
• Intrapersonal
• Musical/Rhythmic

The Dramatically Different Classroom • Christine Laitta & Mark Weakland
Kagan Publishing • 1 (800) WEE CO-OP • www.KaganOnline.com

21

Machine Soundscapes

Groups of students generate ideas for an imaginary machine and then, as a group, perform a soundscape using sounds that they create. In this activity, students use listening skills, think creatively, and work as an ensemble.

Stuff You Need

- A selection of everyday objects, percussive instruments and other instruments
- Recording and playback equipment
- Video: *Wallace and Gromit: A Close Shave* or play any video with a machine
- Audiotape: *The Typewriter* by Leroy Anderson
- Audiotape: *Postage Stamp* a field recording from Ghana

Stuff You Need to Know

In this activity, which is a perfect follow up to Ensemble Activity 7 (Machine), students create a soundscape. A soundscape is a collection of sounds that represent an object or environment. For example, a woodland soundscape could contain wind sounds, insect sounds, bird sounds, students hitting sticks together (a woodpecker?, tree branches scraping?), etc. All sounds should be vocally or instrumentally generated or created from everyday objects. To help speed things along when it is time for the students to share their soundscapes, decide on a performance order with one group always "on deck."

1. Introduction and Discussion

Teacher leads the class in a discussion.
- What is a machine, what is not?
- Could a machine be soundless?
- What do machines sound like?
- What determines the unique sound of a machine?

2. Listen to the Video

If possible, listen to the *Knitting Machine* excerpt from the Wallace and Gromit video. (You may use any video with a machine.) Do not view! Have the students write down their guesses about the purpose of the knitting machine (or other machine) based on the sounds it makes. Now view the video with sound. You may be able to find other audio excerpts of machines, such as the Pink Floyd song "Money" which has a slot machine in the beginning.

3. Discuss the Term "Soundscape"

Use the definition at left to help you with this discussion. You may want to create your own examples of soundscapes to share with the class.

The Dramatically Different Classroom • Christine Laitta & Mark Weakland
Kagan Publishing • 1 (800) WEE CO-OP • www.KaganOnline.com

4. Create a Machine Soundscape

Here are two approaches for small groups:

- First the students decide on a type of machine. Then they develop the sounds for its movements.
- First allow the students to experiment with sounds until they are inspired to create a machine that goes with the sounds.

5. Practice

Students gather in their small groups and take time to organize and perfect their soundscape.

6. Perform and Record

Groups perform without discussing the type or purpose of their machines. After each performance, nonperforming students guess at a name for the machine and a short description of its function.

Enhancers

- Record the soundscapes as the groups perform them. Use in listening center.
- Students participate in a composed "machine," *The Typewriter* by Leroy Anderson. This piece of music uses the sound of a typewriter as the main instrument. This activity can be done with gloves and a black light!
- Students go into their homes or out into the community with a recording device and record machine sounds. The class listens to the excerpts and guesses the function of each machine.

Multiple Intelligences

- Musical/Rhythmic
- Interpersonal
- Verbal/Linguistic
- Bodily/Kinesthetic

The Dramatically Different Classroom • Christine Laitta & Mark Weakland
Kagan Publishing • 1 (800) WEE CO-OP • www.KaganOnline.com

23

Huddle-Up

A team huddle-up (hands-in-the-middle cheer) is a great way to start and end the day. It promotes teamwork, while nurturing class pride.

1. Generate Phrases

Have each student write down a word or a phrase that excites, motivates and generally revs them up.

2. Prepare Mottoes for Class

Review the suggestions and place them in a hat or box that is displayed for the class to see. The hat or box should be easy to access.

3. Students Choose a Motto

Let the students take turns reaching into the hat and choosing the day's motto.

4. Make a Circle

Huddle the class up and have them put their hands in the middle.

5. Explain the Rules

Explain that on the count of three everyone shouts out the the phrase that was picked. "Class 104 is great!"

6. Make It a Part of Your Day

Do it everyday. Start and end each day or class period with a huddle-up.

The Dramatically Different Classroom • Christine Laitta & Mark Weakland
Kagan Publishing • 1 (800) WEE CO-OP • www.KaganOnline.com

Slap-It

Using a slap, students work as a group to pass a rhythm around the table. This activity promotes concentration and rhythm within a group setting.

1. Form a Circle

Have your group sit on the floor or at a table. The students sit with their hands in front of them.

2. Crisscross

- Students start by placing their hands out in front of them with their palms down on the table. Their hands should be slightly to the left and right.
- Pick a student to be first. The person on the student's right should place his left hand under the right hand of the first student. Their hands should cross at the wrist and their hands should be palm down and free to slap the table.
- Continue the pattern all the way around the table until every student has one hand crossed under and one hand crossed over.

3. Set the Rules

- There are three possible movements each student can make: one slap, two slaps, or one knock.
- To start the movements, always traveling counter-clockwise.
- One slap continues the movement in the established direction.
- Two slaps reverses the direction.
- One knock skips the immediate next hand.

4. Practice Makes Perfect

Have your students practice passing the slap around the circle. Students should strive to stay in rhythm.

Stuff You Need

- A large round table big enough for everyone to have their hands on it
- Empty space on the floor (if table is not available)

Stuff You Need to Know

Students sit around a large round table with their hands in front of them. One hand is under and one hand is over the hand of the students on either side of them. Students must keep the rhythm and remember the pattern that is initiated by the teacher.

Enhancers

- Do it faster.
- If you miss the beat, remove that hand from the table.
- If you slap out of turn, remove that hand from the table.
- Try this with your family during the holidays.

Multiple Intelligences

- Bodily/Kinesthetic
- Interpersonal
- Musical/Rhythmic

The Dramatically Different Classroom • Christine Laitta & Mark Weakland
Kagan Publishing • 1 (800) WEE CO-OP • www.KaganOnline.com

25

Bibbity Bop Bop Boo

With the teacher in the middle keeping the beat, the students stand in a circle and rhythmically call out the names and unique qualities of their peers around them. This activity is a great way to introduce students to one another in the first week of school.

Stuff You Need

• Empty space big enough to form a circle that includes everyone in the class

Stuff You Need to Know

This is a great icebreaker for the first week of school because it allows the students to learn about their peers a little bit at a time. It's fun, nonthreatening and it doesn't put any one student on the spot.

1. Explain the Game

Explain to the students that they will form a large circle. The teacher will be in the center. Once in the circle, each student will learn the name of the student to his or her immediate left and right. The teacher will keep a beat going by snapping (1-2-3-4, 1-2-3-4), pointing to a student randomly in the circle, and saying rhythmically, "Left, Bibbity Bop Bop Boo" or "Right, Bibbity Bop Bop Boo." As soon as the teacher points to a student and says "left" or "right," that student must say the name of the person to his or her immediate left or right before the teacher finishes the phrase "Bibbity Bop Bop Boo."

2. Form a Circle

The teacher is in the middle. Let the students stand where they want to, but encourage them to stand next to students they do not know.

3. Start Out Slow

Try to get to each student. You may want to form a pattern, such as skipping every other student or skip two, go back one.

The Dramatically Different Classroom • Christine Laitta & Mark Weakland
Kagan Publishing • 1 (800) WEE CO-OP • www.KaganOnline.com

4. Get Faster, Then Change the Order

As the students catch onto the challenge and begin to learn the names of their peers, increase the speed of the snapping and the "Bibbity Bop Bop Boo." After you have built up to a fast tempo, stop and have the circle reform, once again encouraging the students to stand next to people they don't know.

5. Change the Learning

Instead of learning the names of his or her immediate peers, the student is now responsible for learning one of their favorite things and one of their least favorite things. Give everyone 20 seconds of think time so that they can think of one of their favorite things. Responses should be only one to two words long, such as "friends," "pizza," "bike riding," "my brother" or "Beastie Boys."

Enhancers

- Find other categorical substitutes to learn, such as favorite foods, a unique talent, eye color or favorite musical groups.
- Use this as a review activity for social studies, language arts or science. Instead of saying the name of a peer, each student would have to call out an answer to a specific question, topic or category. For example, if the class is biology and the category is genetics, each student would have to say a word or short phrase about genetics, such as "Mendel," "RNA," "transcription," or "mitosis."

Multiple Intelligences

- Bodily/Kinesthetic
- Interpersonal
- Musical/Rhythmic

*Note: This activity is based on an idea from Ambrose Panico's **Classroom Community**.*

The Dramatically Different Classroom • Christine Laitta & Mark Weakland
Kagan Publishing • 1 (800) WEE CO-OP • www.KaganOnline.com

27

Language Arts
(Readin' & 'Riting)

The Dramatically Different Classroom • Christine Laitta & Mark Weakland
Kagan Publishing • 1 (800) WEE CO-OP • www.KaganOnline.com

29

A Line at a Time

Students orally create a story one line at a time. This activity helps students to listen and process what others are saying. It also works as a sequencing activity.

Stuff You Need

• A clear space to sit your class on the floor

Stuff You Need to Know

This activity promotes one of the main objectives of this book: teaching students to listen in a critical and thoughtful manner.

Enhancers

• We encourage you to tape record the session in order to save your ideas and stories. You (or students) can also transcribe it so that other students can reread the story with more flow and rhythm.
• Once a group gets good, don't pick a topic. Just let the stories unfold.
• First, do this as an oral activity and then use it as a writing activity.
• If you have transcribed the story, print it out and have the students dramatically read them.
• Act out the story.
• Create poems, limericks and haiku one line at a time.
• For a real challenge, have the students create the story ONE WORD AT A TIME!

Multiple Intelligences

• Verbal/Linguistic
• Interpersonal
• Logical/ Mathematical

1. Form a Circle

Get the group in a circle, preferably on the floor. Explain that together you are going to create a story one line at time.

2. Choose a Topic

Agree on a topic. Remind the students that a story needs a beginning, middle and end. For example, our story is about a dog that takes a trip to the store to buy a bone.

3. Create the Opening Line

The teacher begins the story by giving a line, for example "One day a dog named Sparky was hungry." The teacher then asks the student next to her to add the next line. The teacher should side coach the students so that they stay with the plot.

4. Create New Groups

Once the students become comfortable with the process, you may want to break them into two or three groups. This will increase time on task and will create two or three different versions of the story. Later, the students can compare the stories.

30

The Dramatically Different Classroom • Christine Laitta & Mark Weakland
Kagan Publishing • 1 (800) WEE CO-OP • www.KaganOnline.com

The ABC's of Storytelling

Students create a story, one word at a time, using the alphabet as a guideline. This is a challenging activity that stresses listening, creative problem solving, and storytelling. It works best after you have tried other storytelling activities.

Stuff You Need

- An alphabet written or displayed where everyone can see it
- A clear space for everyone to sit in a circle
- ABC Story Guide blackline master

Stuff You Need to Know

The activity has built-in management because it requires thinking prior to speaking. The group must listen for mistakes while planning what they will say when it is their turn.

1. Form a Circle

Sit the group in a circle. Explain that together the class will create a story using the alphabet as a guideline.

2. Give Examples

Model an example for the group.
- *Annie bought cabbages during Edward's Friday gala.*
- *A boisterous clown danced excitedly for Gail. How incredible!*

3. Create a Story

Create a story out loud by taking turns adding a word. See how far you can go. You may want to have "safety" cards; small words such as to, the, and, those. These cards help students when they get stuck.

Enhancers

- Bring it down a grade level. Have the children begin each sentence with a word that follows the sequence of the alphabet. For example: Amy bought a car. Betty drove it home.
- Start in the middle of the alphabet and work back to the letter that you started from.
- Take the alphabet away and do the activity from memory. The teacher will listen for mistakes.
- Have your students do the activity in cooperative groups of three to five students.
- Do this activity in pairs and try having a dialogue with a classmate, either a letter at a time or a phrase at a time.
- You may want to have the students write their stories and conversation. This helps them to create the story more easily and it functions as a writing activity.

Multiple Intelligences

- Verbal/Linguistic
- Interpersonal

The Dramatically Different Classroom • Christine Laitta & Mark Weakland
Kagan Publishing • 1 (800) WEE CO-OP • www.KaganOnline.com

31

ABC Story Guide

Name_____ Date_____

A _____   N _____

B _____   O _____

C _____   P _____

D _____   Q _____

E _____   R _____

F _____   S _____

G _____   T _____

H _____   U _____

I _____   V _____

J _____   W _____

K _____   X _____

L _____   Y _____

M _____   Z _____

The Dramatically Different Classroom • Christine Laitta & Mark Weakland
Kagan Publishing • 1 (800) WEE CO-OP • www.KaganOnline.com

Story Theater

Students and the teacher collaborate to act out a story. As the reader, the teacher is in control of the pace and mood of the story and acts as the side coach. Story comprehension, sequencing, and working as an ensemble are taught in this activity.

1. Read the Story

Teacher and students read through the story.

2. Discuss the Story

Discuss the main ideas and characters of the story. Choose the characters and the students who will portray them. The other students will be involved in the story when they create the environment through the use of story sounds, locations and objects.

3. Teach Them Their Cues

Remind the students that as you read the story, the class will act it out and will change the mood, the setting and the characters' relationships with one another as the story unfolds.

4. Rehearse the Sticky Situations

Before reading the story for the second time, practice creating the best ways to represent characters, locations, environments, and events. You are not practicing the whole story! For example, when reading *The Rainbow Fish*, the class practices how they will work together to become an octopus, moving and speaking together, with fluid motions.

5. Share the Story

Act out the story for another class.

Stuff You Need

• A great story with lots of characters
• A space to move around in
• Stories that leave lots to the imagination

Stuff You Need to Know

Side coachings are gentle reminders during the telling of the story that help to keep the student on the right track as they act out the part. Here is an example from *Where the Wild Things Are*:
Reader: *An ocean tumbled by*
Side Coach: *Lets make ocean noises now, waves crashing*
Reader: *With a private boat for Max*
Side Coach: *Join hands and make your boat*

Enhancers

• Have the students write their own stories, share them with others and work out ways to perform them.
• Make this lesson cross-curricular by creating costumes in art class and recording sounds and music in music class.

Multiple Intelligences

• Verbal/Linguistic
• Interpersonal
• Bodily/Kinesthetic
• Logical/Mathematical
• Musical/Rhythmic

The Dramatically Different Classroom • Christine Laitta & Mark Weakland
Kagan Publishing • 1 (800) WEE CO-OP • www.KaganOnline.com

33

The Talk Back Talk Show

In this activity, students review their language arts lesson by creating and participating in a talk show. This makes the abstract concrete by turning words on paper into dramatic, real-life action. This is a great way to prep students for an exam without saying "read and review your chapters."

Stuff You Need

• One chair per talk show guest
• A list of student-and teacher-generated questions about current topic of study

Stuff You Need to Know

Did you know that people such as Oprah Winfrey and Rosie O'Donnell are very recognizable and highly interesting to children? Students respond well to TV-based activities because they are so familiar with the medium.

1. Produce Your Own Talk Show

Create a talk show set by placing a few chairs in the front of the room. The rest of the class will be an audience and you will serve as the host (and the control!)

2. Divide Students Into Groups

Some students will be guests and some will be the studio audience, but everyone will have to prepare questions. The guests are based on what students are studying. The guests could be characters in novels, grammar and punctuation. So if the class is having a test on how to use punctuation, the guests are Chris Comma, Suzy Semicolon, and Pete Period. The students then prepare and ask questions of the guests. Questions can be pulled from the text and review sections, but encourage the students to come up with ones that synthesize information and go beyond just the facts. For example, "Chris, when is the best time to use you in a sentence?"

The Dramatically Different Classroom • Christine Laitta & Mark Weakland
Kagan Publishing • 1 (800) WEE CO-OP • www.KaganOnline.com

- If you have older and/or mature students, let them be the host.
- Take commercial breaks. These can be bathroom breaks or even a spelling quiz. If you are more ambitious, create an ad that coincides with the talk show. For example, write a commercial that promotes Nibbler's Rodent Food (loved by all pet mice everywhere!) or a bookstore chain promoting John Steinbeck Week.
- Challenge kids to become "experts." After finding additional information on the author, era or characters, they can appear on the show as a professor of literature.
- How about doing this just for fun? You can do this activity at homeroom parties or as a reward. Have the kids pick a Disney character or someone from a fairy tale. These characters will now be the talk show guests. Add costumes if possible.
- You can apply this activity to science (scientists as guests or elements from the periodic chart) or health (organs appear as guests).

3. Review the Panel's Questions

Prior to picking the guests, have the students review the questions with one another and practice answering them (although the students don't know it, they are reviewing for their test). The better they know the information, the better they will be as guests.

4. Select Your Guests

If you are studying one subject, pick multiple guests to be the same subject. If you are studying a book or a concept, choose several students to be different aspects of the concept or different characters in the book. For example, if you are reading *Of Mice and Men*, pick one student to be Lenny and another to be Curly. If you are reading, *The Mouse and the Motorcycle* pick one student to be the mouse Ralph, one to be Keith, one to be Matt, and one to be Ralph's mother.

Multiple Intelligences

- Verbal/Linguistic
- Interpersonal
- Bodily/Kinesthetic

The Dramatically Different Classroom • Christine Laitta & Mark Weakland
Kagan Publishing • 1 (800) WEE CO-OP • www.KaganOnline.com

35

Sounding Out Your Story

Students create sounds that enhance a story as it is read aloud by the teacher or other students. This activity allows students to demonstrate their knowledge of the story's characters and plot. It helps students develop listening skills and increase attention spans.

Stuff You Need

- Short stories with repetitive plot lines and characters, for example: *The Napping House* by Audrey Wood, *The Very Quiet Cricket* by Eric Carle, *Legend of the Persian Carpet*, or *Why Mosquitoes Buzz*
- Story Sounds blackline master

Stuff You Need to Know

This is a fun and creative way to spice up a reading class. Encourage students to create lines of dialogue, fun sounds and/or specific words to represent the characters.

Enhancers

- Break into small cooperative groups to assign sounds to the story. Next read the story with the sounds. Then meet as a class and compare what sounds were used and why.
- Have your children write their own sound stories, either independently, with a partner or in cooperative groups!
- Children who have difficulty with reading and writing can write or read simple stories, listen carefully and do the sound effects as the teacher reads, or be assigned the role of sound designer or sound maker when working in small groups.

Multiple Intelligences

- Verbal/Linguistic
- Interpersonal
- Logical/Mathematical
- Musical/Rhythmic

1. Choose a Story

Pick a short story that has repeating characters and events. Fairy tales are good stories to use.

2. Create a Sound

Have the students assign sound effects to characters, events or actions. The sounds should be based on the meaning of the event and action or the trait of the character. The students should focus on words and phrases that are repeated throughout the text.
Examples:
King=trumpet fanfare
Magic Troll="Hee, hee, hee"
Evil Queen="Off with their heads"
happy="yea"
distressed="ohh, woe is me!"
 waved his sword="ssswwishhh!"

3. Add Your Sounds

The teacher reads the story aloud. Each time the character, action or event is read, the students must make the sound that has been assigned.
For example:

Once there was a king ("fanfare") who was kindhearted and happy ("yeah!"), but his wife the queen ("off with their heads") was a mean and nasty woman. In fact, the queen ("off with their heads"), whom no one liked, was really an evil witch in disguise.

36

The Dramatically Different Classroom • Christine Laitta & Mark Weakland
Kagan Publishing • 1 (800) WEE CO-OP • www.KaganOnline.com

Story Sounds

Name_____ Date_____

List the name of the story character or event on the left. On the right, list the sound that will be made each time the character's name or story event is read out loud.

Character	Sound
_____	_____
_____	_____
_____	_____
_____	_____

Action	Sound
_____	_____
_____	_____

Special Word	Sound
_____	_____
_____	_____

The Dramatically Different Classroom • Christine Laitta & Mark Weakland
Kagan Publishing • 1 (800) WEE CO-OP • www.KaganOnline.com

37

Sound Effect Stories

Students create a wordless story using sounds. As they use sound effects, students practice sequencing and solve the problem of how to communicate without using words. This activity gives students with undeveloped writing and oral communication skills a chance to tell a story and express themselves.

Stuff You Need

• Instruments or objects that make interesting sounds

Stuff You Need to Know

Remind the students that even though the story is made up of a few short sounds, it still has to have a beginning, a middle and an end.

Enhancers

• Break into small groups or partners and have them work cooperatively to create a sound story based on cue cards or a story they have written.
• Record the sound stories on audiotape.
• Write a brief synopsis of each sound story on an index card. After listening to each story, students pick the card that goes with the sound story.

Multiple Intelligences

• Verbal/Linguistic
• Interpersonal
• Logical/Mathematical
• Musical/Rhythmic

1. Prepare Teaching Aids

Place a group of musical instruments and classroom objects on a table or desk.

2. Explain the Rules

The teacher explains that she will tell a story by using only sounds made from objects or sounds created by the teacher herself. No words will be used.

3. Teacher Models

Teacher models a story.
For example:
• Taps fingers on table (pitter, patter, pitter, patter).
• Makes a squeak (squeak!).
• Taps fingers again (pitter, patter, pitter, patter).
• Smacks lips (smack, smack!).
Our story is about a mouse that finds some cheese, squeaks in glee and eats the cheese.

4. Adapt Your Lesson

Based on the ability of the individual student, do one of the following:
• Let the student create a story on the spot by choosing four sounds.
• Using cue cards that outline the plot of a short story, allow the student to pick sounds that would tell the story.
• Using cue cards that outline the plot of a short story, give the student the sounds that tell a story and have him perform the sound story.

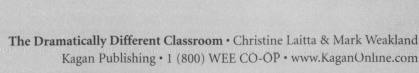

The Dramatically Different Classroom • Christine Laitta & Mark Weakland
Kagan Publishing • 1 (800) WEE CO-OP • www.KaganOnline.com

Character Monologues

Students write and perform a monologue. By creating a monologue, the students demonstrate comprehension of a character in a fictional story, a biography or an autobiography. This activity actually brings the characters to life.

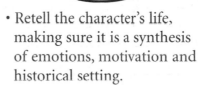

1. Discuss

Explain what a monologue is and model examples from books and videos.

2. Choose a Character

Help students choose a character. In a biography or autobiography, this is easy! If you are doing a biography theme, you can either have everyone read a book about a different person or have everyone read about and become the same person.

3. Explain the Objective

Help students focus on their monologue's topic by setting parameters, ranging from the concrete to the abstract. Here are some examples:

- Retell the character's life and cover all the major events.
- Tell about a specific life event. What happened? How did he or she feel about it? How did it impact on the rest of his or her life?

- Retell the character's life, making sure it is a synthesis of emotions, motivation and historical setting.
- Discuss how it feels to be living in the era in which the character lives.

4. Create an Outline

The students should read their book carefully and then draw up an outline of their monologue. Then they should write their monologue in the first person. (You may need to model this.) The student should become that person.

Stuff You Need

- Examples of people acting out monologues, such as in a school play or from a video clip
- Examples of monologues from a book or a play
- Monologue Rubrics & Evaluation Questions blackline master

Stuff You Need to Know

This activity takes the place of the typical book report.

Enhancers

- Come up with a rubric that critiques the class or use the one provided. How did the delivery of the monologues compare to each other and how did they differ? Using a rubric to critique classmates (in a kind and fair way) during the monologue can really increase their attention to each other's presentations.
- Pick two characters and have them comment on the same event in a story. Points of view must be defensible by the story's content.
- Videotape the biographies and air them on your public access channel!
- Try presenting a monologue under the heading, "The biggest challenge of my life."

Multiple Intelligences

- Verbal/Linguistic
- Interpersonal
- Logical/ Mathematical
- Musical/ Rhythmic
- Bodily/Kinesthetic

The Dramatically Different Classroom • Christine Laitta & Mark Weakland
Kagan Publishing • 1 (800) WEE CO-OP • www.KaganOnline.com

39

Monologue Rubrics & Evaluation Questions

Sample Rubric: Students Evaluating Students (beginning)

Reads with appropriate expression . . . All the time . . . . . . .Some time . . . . . .Rarely
Uses a loud and clear voice . . . All the time . . . . . . .Some time . . . . . .Rarely
Stance/Posture . . . Very good . . . . .Good . . . . .Needs Improving
Uses Props . . . Yes . . . . .No

Comments: _____

Sample Rubric: Teacher Evaluating Students

Reads with expression . . . All the time . . . . . . .Some time . . . . . .Rarely
Uses a loud and clear voice . . . All the time . . . . . . .Some time . . . . . .Rarely
Stance/Posture . . . Excellent . . . . .Needs Improving
Uses Props . . . Yes . . . . .No
Details of Character's Life . . . In depth . . . . .General . . . . .Needs more
Impact . . . Believable . . . . . . .Somewhat . . . . . .Not

Comments: _____

Evaluation: Students and Teacher Evaluating Students (middle/high school)

• Did the person choose information that made you stop and think? If yes, what information?
• Did the character move you? If yes, what did they do and why did it affect you?
• Did the person give a dramatic presentation? If yes, what did you like? If no, what could he/she have done better?
• Do you feel like you now have an understanding of the person's life? Why or why not?

Comments: _____

Sample Evaluation of Presentations: Students and Teachers Evaluating Students

• Evaluations should be made in terms of what the student was working toward.
• Did you believe what they were saying and was it done with conviction?
• Did you understand the goals, dreams and motivations of the character or person?
• Was there conflict, either inner conflict or conflict with others?
• Was there evidence of preparation? Did the presenter know their character's past and did they use that information in their presentation?
• If there are two or more presenters at the same time, did they listen to one another and play off of each other?
• Was there a sense of progression? Did the character in the monologue change?
• Was there physical or vocal tension?

The Dramatically Different Classroom • Christine Laitta & Mark Weakland
Kagan Publishing • 1 (800) WEE CO-OP • www.KaganOnline.com

Readin', Rhymin' & Rhythm

In this activity, the student memorizes a story by listening to it. Each student becomes familiar with the written words by watching the teacher point to them as the stories are chanted or sung. This activity reinforces basic reading skills, thereby helping emerging or beginning readers.

1. Choose a Poem

Choose a simple poem or a children's book that has rhyming words and repeated text. If you want to first sing the story or poem, choose a story that comes from a song, such as:

- *There Was An Old Lady; Knickknack Paddy Whack; London Bridge; What a Beautiful World; Chicken Soup With Rice; There Ain't No Bugs; John Brown's Body*

Or break out your old campfire song book! Here are more ideas:

- *Ol' Dan Tucker; Froggy Went a Courtin'; He's Got the Whole World in His Hands*

Here are some suggestions for stories that can be chanted:

- *Chick a Chick a Boom Boom; Fire, Fire; Over in the Meadow; Old Mother Hubbard*

2. Practice Chanting It as an Ensemble

Put the text on big easel paper and either chant it out, starting slowly, or sing it. If you have chosen a poem, simply chant it out.

3. Test for Word Recognition

After you have sung and/or chanted the stories, songs and poems over the course of a number of days, test for word recognition by asking for a volunteer to come up and point to specific words. Place words on separate cards and check the students to see if they can remember the words out of context.

4. Check Again

You can also test for generalization by combining words from different songs, chants and poems into a single sentence.
Example: The old lady liked to walk by beautiful London Bridge.

Stuff You Need

- Books
- Large sheets of paper or easel paper

Stuff You Need to Know

Many children who lack basic reading skills or have a limited ability to read can gain word recognition by singing or chanting stories written on large sheets of easel paper. While reading, remember to use a strong beat.

Enhancers

- You can chant spelling rules, lists of pronouns, science statements and math formulas on a regular basis. The most important things to remember are to use rhyme and rhythm and to repeat the chant on a daily basis.
  - Brainstorm a list of books that are engaging and full of rhymes. Consult with your school's reading specialist, special education teacher and librarian for lots of ideas.

Multiple Intelligences

- Verbal/Linguistic
- Interpersonal
- Musical/Rhythmic

The Dramatically Different Classroom • Christine Laitta & Mark Weakland
Kagan Publishing • 1 (800) WEE CO-OP • www.KaganOnline.com

41

Re-creating the Classics

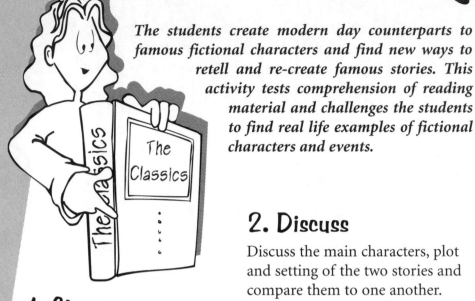

The students create modern day counterparts to famous fictional characters and find new ways to retell and re-create famous stories. This activity tests comprehension of reading material and challenges the students to find real life examples of fictional characters and events.

Stuff You Need

- Books containing classic stories
- Re-created Story blackline master

Stuff You Need to Know

Before they can compare and contrast the similarities between history, literature and the arts, the students must be able to comprehend the subtext of the material.

Enhancers

- Have the students pick a scene from their new version and write a script so they can act it out and then video tape it.
- Question the students: Who would be a modern Humpty Dumpty? Who would be a modern day Giving Tree? (Mother Theresa, Dalai Lama or someone in the students' own lives!) Challenge your students to take a fictitious character and find its modern, real life counterpart.
- Listen to their language: Be open to the words and reasoning of the students. If they can justify their choice and support their feeling with concrete plausible details, then they've got it!

Multiple Intelligences

- Verbal/Linguistic
- Interpersonal
- Bodily/Kinesthetic
- Intrapersonal

1. Choose Your Story

Pick a famous book that contains a timeless idea that your students are familiar with. For example, *Romeo and Juliet* tells of the love of one person for another who is outside of his social class. Then discuss how the story has been transferred into a modern day setting, in this case, *West Side Story*. Other examples of transference are Joseph Conrad's *Heart of Darkness* retold in Francis Ford Coppola's *Apocalypse Now* or Shakespeare's *Taming of the Shrew* re-created as the musical *Kiss Me Kate*.

2. Discuss

Discuss the main characters, plot and setting of the two stories and compare them to one another.

3. Provide a List

Provide your students with a list of historical stories or characters that they are familiar with, such as *King Lear*, *Othello*, *The Boy Who Cried Wolf*, *Sarah Plain and Tall*, *The Glass Menagerie* and *The Great Gatsby*. Adapt the books for the age level and ability level of the students.

4. Students Write a Modern Day Version

Have the entire class write an alternate, modern day version of the story or event. Show the relationships between the traditional characters and the new characters. Now, in small groups act out the original and the revised versions.

The Dramatically Different Classroom • Christine Laitta & Mark Weakland
Kagan Publishing • 1 (800) WEE CO-OP • www.KaganOnline.com

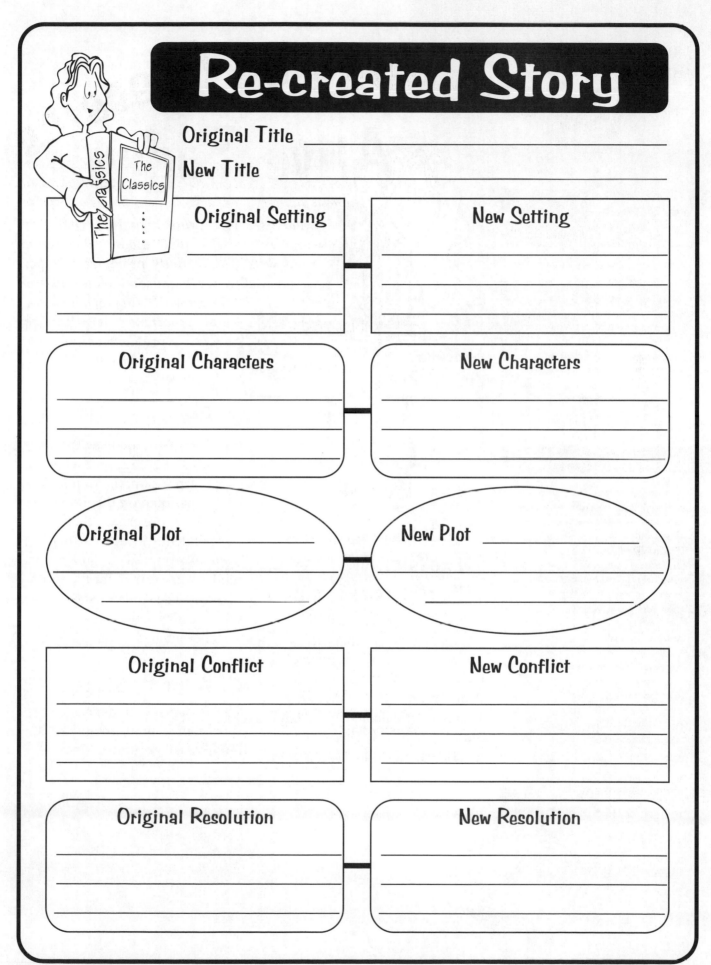

Re-created Story

Original Title _____

New Title _____

Original Setting
_____
_____
_____

New Setting
_____
_____
_____

Original Characters
_____
_____
_____

New Characters
_____
_____
_____

Original Plot _____
_____
_____

New Plot _____
_____
_____

Original Conflict
_____
_____
_____

New Conflict
_____
_____
_____

Original Resolution
_____
_____
_____

New Resolution
_____
_____
_____

The Dramatically Different Classroom • Christine Laitta & Mark Weakland
Kagan Publishing • 1 (800) WEE CO-OP • www.KaganOnline.com

43

If They Were Alive Today

Students revive famous literary characters and events with their modern-day scripts and skits. This activity promotes intrapersonal intelligences because students pull from their own library of knowledge and experience. It allows for creative problem solving and tests comprehension.

Stuff You Need

• A group of historical figures the students are familiar with.

Stuff You Need to Know

The students need as much information as possible about the people or events. Encourage the students to research in various ways, such as asking family members, using the internet, and accessing the arts and music section of their local library.

Salem Witch Trials   McCarthyism

Enhancers

• Videotape it. Did we mention that taking pictures and shooting video are great management devices?
• Question the students: Who would be a modern day Eleanor Roosevelt or Andrew Carnegie?
• Question the students: What book, story or poem might reflect the discovery of the new world? (*Where the Wild Things Are* by Maurice Sendak)
• Challenge the students to take a historical event and find a modern-day counterpart from a story, movie or TV show.
• Encourage the students to find a historical figure who has qualities similar to themselves.

1. Choose Two Similar Characters or Events

The teacher picks a historical character or event that the students are familiar with and then shows its modern day equivalent. An example of an event would be the Salem Witch Trials and McCarthyism. These events are also examined in *The Crucible*.

2. Provide a List

Provide your students with a list of historical events, such as the Great Depression, the Inquisition, or the first man on the moon. Have the entire class, either independently, with a partner or in small groups, write an alternate, modern-day version of the story or event. The students show the relationships between the traditional event and the new event.

3. Write It, Share It

The students write their new version in script form and act it out in small groups.

Multiple Intelligences

• Verbal/Linguistic
• Interpersonal
• Logical/ Mathematical
• Musical/Rhythmic
• Bodily/Kinesthetic
• Intrapersonal

44

A Real Life Fairy Tale

Students create modern-day fairy tales, fables, or nursery rhymes with messages that address modern-day problems and conflicts. This activity teaches the students the meaning of subtext, promotes the use of intrapersonal intelligence, and teaches higher-level reading and writing skills.

1. Review the Subtext

Define subtext for your students. Subtext is the underlying meaning or theme of a story, or the true meaning of what the author is saying. Read two or three fairy tales with your students and discuss the subtext of the story. For example, the subtext of *Cinderella* or *The Ugly Duckling* is that although people may put you down because of your station in life or the way you look, and though you may start to see yourself as others see you, when given time to grow you will blossom into the beautiful person you truly are.

2. Discuss Fairy Tales

Discuss how fairy tales were used to teach society proper ways to interact and deal with problems. Point out that their messages were effective because they were delivered in an interesting way.

3. Tell Your Tale

Once they have an understanding of where the tales come from and what human conditions they speak to, encourage the students to write their own fairy tales based on a modern day problem. Remind them to use interesting, fantastic, and/or magical elements to tell their tales. They can work individually or in small groups to do this and can write the tale in any way they choose, such as a script, a poem, or a narrative.

4. Act It Out, Discuss

If the tale is written as a narrative, the students can go back to Story Theater (Activity 3) where they choose people to portray the characters while the teacher side coaches. Students act out the tale and discuss it.

Stuff You Need

• Books of fairy tales, fables and nursery rhymes to use as references

Stuff You Need to Know

When given the opportunity to express themselves, students are able to create many solutions to present-day problems. Challenge the groups to create a new set of stories for today's generation.

Enhancers

• Publish the new fairy tales. Illustrate them.
• Invite other classes and other people to come and share as the students bring their fairy tales to life.

Multiple Intelligences

• Verbal/Linguistic
• Interpersonal
• Intrapersonal

The Dramatically Different Classroom • Christine Laitta & Mark Weakland
Kagan Publishing • 1 (800) WEE CO-OP • www.KaganOnline.com

45

Radio Theater

Students produce and act in an old-fashioned radio drama. This activity allows students to work in an ensemble, exercise both logic and creativity, and use musical, interpersonal and verbal intelligences.

Stuff You Need

- The original recording of *The War of the Worlds* or a recent version of it, or any other radio drama
- Tape recorder
- Selection of noise-making props
- Radio Drama Outline blackline master

Stuff You Need to Know

This lesson is based on Orson Wells' famous radio drama, *The War of the Worlds*. You should discuss the background of this historic radio presentation and its effects on many Americans. You should also discuss the importance of radio as a source of entertainment and information.

Enhancers

- Add an old-time radio as a prop.
- Hide the performers behind a screen.
- If possible, have them speak through a microphone and amplifier.
- Have the students write their own radio program. It should be short, but it must contain a beginning, middle and end. They may also want to include a commercial.

Multiple Intelligences

- Verbal/Linguistic
- Interpersonal
- Logical/Mathematical
- Intrapersonal
- Musical/Rhythmic

1. Review the History of Radio

After reviewing the background of radio, introduce the characters of the radio drama by either passing out a summary of the characters or simply listing them on the board and discussing them.

2. Play Out the Story Until the Climax

Play *The War of the Worlds* up to the point where the hatch of the mysterious cylinder from Mars is about to open. Then stop the tape! At this point in the story, the announcer is about to reveal what is emerging from the cylinder. (You can use any radio drama. Stop tape before the climax.)

3. And Then...

Brainstorm what happens next and list the possible conclusions to the story.

4. Make It Happen

Form cooperative groups and let them finish the drama. Use the blackline as a planning form. They should write at least one version of the drama's ending in the form of a script. Encourage them to be true to the original drama's mood and sound. They will need to decide on how and when to use sound effects. Give ample time to create and practice the drama.

5. Share the New Endings

Present each group's exciting conclusion. Use the "on-deck" method so that the next group is ready to go as soon as the prior group finishes.

The Dramatically Different Classroom • Christine Laitta & Mark Weakland
Kagan Publishing • 1 (800) WEE CO-OP • www.KaganOnline.com

Radio Drama Outline

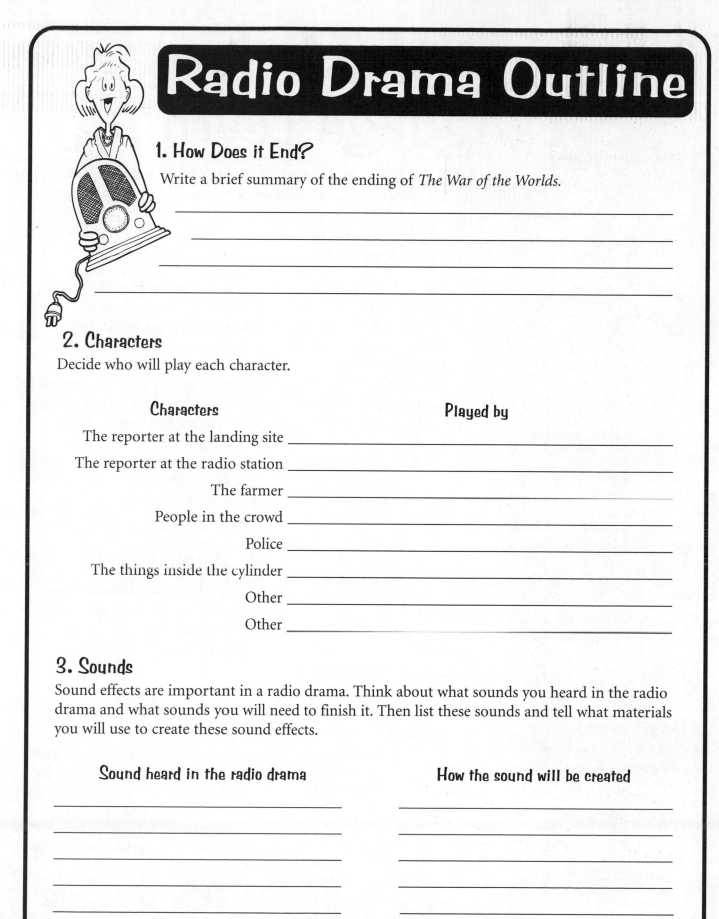

1. How Does it End?

Write a brief summary of the ending of *The War of the Worlds*.

_____

_____

_____

_____

2. Characters

Decide who will play each character.

Characters	Played by
The reporter at the landing site	_____
The reporter at the radio station	_____
The farmer	_____
People in the crowd	_____
Police	_____
The things inside the cylinder	_____
Other	_____
Other	_____

3. Sounds

Sound effects are important in a radio drama. Think about what sounds you heard in the radio drama and what sounds you will need to finish it. Then list these sounds and tell what materials you will use to create these sound effects.

Sound heard in the radio drama	How the sound will be created
_____	_____
_____	_____
_____	_____
_____	_____
_____	_____

The Dramatically Different Classroom • Christine Laitta & Mark Weakland
Kagan Publishing • 1 (800) WEE CO-OP • www.KaganOnline.com

47

Music for Language Learning

Use music as a springboard into a lesson or to supplement a lesson, thereby aiding in the retention of factual information.

1. Songs to Get You Started

Here are ideas that help you enhance existing lessons by adding music. The following is a small list of songs and ideas to get you started:

• **Grammar:** *Conjunction Junction* from School House Rock. Any song from School House Rock works great in the classroom.

• **Phonics:** *The TION Song* from the Electric Company; *Silent E* by Tom Lehrer; *Sammy the Snake* from Sesame Street.

• **Chants/Raps:** *Rap It Up* by Mark Weakland (cheap promo!). Available from Academic Communications Associates.

• **Biography:** Marian Anderson-spirituals, excerpts from her operas contrasted with The Who's *Tommy*, a rock opera by Pete Townsend; the music of Puerto Rico when studying Roberto Clemente; *Starry, Starry Night* by Don McClean when studying Vincent van Gogh

• **Literature:** When studying Hemingway's *Old Man and the Sea*; *The Ocean* by Led Zeppelin; *Ocean Dream* by Paul Winter; *Mood Music* (the sound of waves crashing)

• **Language Arts:** *Ironic* by Alanis Morissette

• **Writing:** Put on music that expresses strong emotions like *Night On Bald Mountain* and *Smells Like Teen Spirit* by Nirvana or Beethoven's *Moonlight Sonata*. Have the students write what they are feeling and hearing. For a reward or something a little different, play ambient or mood music in the background as the students write.

2. Collect Songs

Talk to the students about their ideas for songs. Also consult with other teachers and the school's music educator.

3. Create a Song Library

Gather songs on either disc or tape and create your own song library and file it under each subject. Unfortunately, we can't give you modern-day choices because we've ceased to listen to music since 1980 (we still think James Taylor is "edgy"). We encourage you to pick hip songs that will speak to your students.

Stuff You Need

• A tape recorder or CD player
• A collection of music

Stuff You Need to Know

Music speaks to the soul and mind and adds levity and life to any lesson.

Enhancers

• Sing along.
• Make up your own educational songs.

Multiple Intelligences

• Verbal/Linguistic
• Interpersonal
• Musical/Rhythmic
• Intrapersonal

The Dramatically Different Classroom • Christine Laitta & Mark Weakland
Kagan Publishing • 1 (800) WEE CO-OP • www.KaganOnline.com

A Picture Is Worth a Thousand Words

Students take a photo or a picture from a magazine and decide what happened prior to the image being taken and what happened immediately after. Students then create a complete story based upon this single picture or image. This activity encourages students to think outside of the box and allows for creative writing and self-expression.

1. Collect Pictures

Collect a number of pictures, historic images, and family photos. Discuss with the class what the photos say. What are their importance? What emotions do they elicit? What stories do they tell?

2. Create a Scenario

Have the students choose a picture and brainstorm on the story behind the picture. Ask what events happened prior to and after the picture was taken.

3. Students Write Their Stories

Have the students write down their stories in either a script or narrative form. Encourage the students to be descriptive.

4. Share

Share the final product with the class by acting out the stories.

Stuff You Need

• An assortment of pictures and photos free of any words or advertisements (one per student)

Stuff You Need to Know

Pictures are a powerful way to save a moment in time. We said it before and we'll say it again, "a picture is worth a thousand words." This can be done as a group or individual activity.

Enhancers

• Create a multisensory show where the students use slides of their image, dialogue and movements to create a complete production.
• Take your students to an art museum.

Multiple Intelligences

• Verbal/Linguistic
• Interpersonal
• Logical/Mathematical
• Bodily/Kinesthetic

The Dramatically Different Classroom • Christine Laitta & Mark Weakland
Kagan Publishing • 1 (800) WEE CO-OP • www.KaganOnline.com

49

The Missing Middle

Students are given the beginning and end of a story or event in a story. Their task is to come up with the missing middle. This summarization activity quickly develops communication and sequencing skills by giving students the opportunity to verbally fill in missing information. It can be used to assess students' knowledge in lieu of a formal test or quiz.

Stuff You Need

• Two events that bracket a time in a story
Here is an example:
STUDENT ONE A family starts on vacation.
STUDENT TWO The family ends up in the wrong location.
• For older students, use two relevant dialogue lines. These are written on two slips of paper

Stuff You Need to Know

The events that are used in this activity can be generated by the teacher, the students or pulled from a book.

Enhancers

• Present the sequence to the class as a dramatic staged reading. This presentation works just as well for narrative as it does for dialogue.

Multiple Intelligences

• Verbal/Linguistic
• Interpersonal
• Logical/Mathematical
• Bodily/Kinesthetic

1. Teacher Pairs Up Students

The teacher pairs up the students and gives them the beginning and end of an event. Once the students are comfortable with this activity, you can have the students generate the beginning and ending events on their own.

For example:
Beginning – Willy Wonka shows the children the river of chocolate.
End – Augustus Gloop has disappeared.

2. Students Uncover Facts

Let the students use any resource to find the missing events. Remind the students to stick to the main events.

3. Students Share Missing Material

The students then share the missing events, motivations and/or dialogue. The dialogue doesn't need to be verbatim (unless that is part of the lesson).

4. Discuss and Critique

Discuss with the class. Is there anything they left out, such as emotions, facts, sequence or motivations? Did they choose significant events?

The Dramatically Different Classroom • Christine Laitta & Mark Weakland
Kagan Publishing • 1 (800) WEE CO-OP • www.KaganOnline.com

What's Your Sign?

Starting with just a few words, the students and teacher learn sign language. Signing, which gives students a chance to use their bodily/kinesthetic intelligence, provides a way to communicate silently in the classroom. It also provides for a break in the day that is both fun and educational.

Stuff You Need

- A good book on signing, such as *Signing Exact English*, published by Modern Signs Press
- The word for each sign placed on a piece of poster board (optional)
- Check the Web for signing resources

Stuff You Need to Know

Children love signing! Many find it to be secretive and mysterious and they love using their hands to express themselves. Signing actively engages both the mind and the body. Start with a few signs that you can teach yourself. Use special educators, speech/language clinicians and even music educators, who often use signs to accompany songs, as resources. Signing can be used in a number of different ways:

- As a short, planned activity at the end of the day
- As a break in the middle of a block
- As a way to start the day
- As an alternate way to teach vocabulary words during language arts class

1. Find Time

Find a regular time to teach and practice signing. You only need a five or ten minute block of time.

2. Teach a Sign

Start with a couple of words. The teacher should pick words that are easy to learn and can be used frequently throughout the day, such as bathroom, sorry, great, stop, talking, drink.

3. Review

Review the signs every day. If the students review all of the previously learned signs and learn a few new ones every day, they will quickly acquire a vocabulary of 50 to 60 signs. Constant review helps to establish "muscle memory."

Enhancers

- Learn a song, such as *Kumbayah* and its accompanying signs then teach it to your class.
- Challenge your students to learn more signs on their own. They can then teach each other or teach the class.

Multiple Intelligences

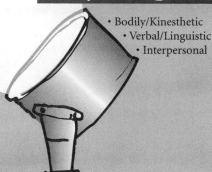

- Bodily/Kinesthetic
- Verbal/Linguistic
- Interpersonal

The Dramatically Different Classroom • Christine Laitta & Mark Weakland
Kagan Publishing • 1 (800) WEE CO-OP • www.KaganOnline.com

51

Poetry Soundscapes

Students dramatically read a poem, perform the poem with sounds that they create and finally evaluate the aesthetic success of their poetry soundscape. This activity promotes musical and compositional creativity, appeals to students with musical intelligence, and engages students who have difficulty with self-expression.

Stuff You Need

- Master poem copy: *little man* by e.e. cummings, *Stopping by the Woods* by Robert Frost, or *Song of Myself* by Walt Whitman (you may prefer another poem)
- Poems for small groups, either selected published poems and/or student-generated
- Highlighter sets of different colors (one set per group)
- Recording and playback equipment: microphones, stands, tape deck, and tapes
- Variety of sound-making objects and small percussion instruments

Stuff You Need to Know

Sounds add drama to the reading of a poem. They can also be a lot of fun for the students.

1. Read and Discuss

The teacher reads a poem without expression and the class analyzes the reading of the poem in order to discover what the missing elements are. We suggest using the poem *little man* by e.e. cummings, but you can pick any poem that suits you and your class.

2. Add Expression

The teacher divides the stanzas of the poem among volunteers. These students read their stanza to the class and add the missing expressive elements, such as rhythm, tempo, and inflection.

3. Sound Off

The class suggests and adds accompanying sounds to the reading. For example, as a volunteer reads the passage "the wind howls," the rest of the class makes soft howling sounds under the reading.

4. Move It

The class gives suggestions to the volunteers on adding movement that would enhance the reading of the poem. Stage the poem by adding movement.

The Dramatically Different Classroom • Christine Laitta & Mark Weakland
Kagan Publishing • 1 (800) WEE CO-OP • www.KaganOnline.com

5. What Was Good?

Evaluate and discuss as a group.

6. On Your Own

Divide the class into small groups or pairs, set the rules, give every group a practice area and provide basic rubrics to the students. Assign them the e.e. cummings poem or a poem of your choice and allow them to divide the poem as they see fit. They then expressively read it, stage it and add appropriate sound effects. The teacher supervises and provides guided practice time.

7. Do It

When groups are ready, decide on a performance order and establish an "on-deck" location so that the performances move. Decide on rubrics before the performance takes place, then perform and record! Critique the work.

Enhancers

- Videotape the performances.
- Allow students to rework (on their own time) and rerecord a performance.
- Set a poem to music.
- Put tape or disk of recorded works in a learning or listening center.

Multiple Intelligences

- Verbal/Linguistic
- Bodily/Kinesthetic
- Musical/Rhythmic
- Interpersonal
- Intrapersonal

The Dramatically Different Classroom • Christine Laitta & Mark Weakland
Kagan Publishing • 1 (800) WEE CO-OP • www.KaganOnline.com

53

Feelings, Nothing More Than...

Students pick a feeling from a feelings list, write a poem about that feeling, and choose or create sounds that represent that feeling. This activity teaches creative writing, self-expression, the power of sound, and teamwork.

Stuff You Need

- Pencil and recycled paper for sketches
- Pens and composition paper for sketches
- Instruments, variety of sound-making objects, small percussion instruments
- Feelings blackline master
- Metaphors & Similes blackline master
- The Feelings Rubric blackline master

Stuff You Need to Know

The Feelings vocabulary handout is a list of many different and subtle feelings one can experience. The page included with this activity is only a partial list of feeling words. The students will need to know what a metaphor and simile are. If they do not know what they are, use the blackline master to teach the concepts. If the students are already familiar with these terms, review or reinforce metaphor and simile in step #4 of the activity.

1. Brainstorm Feelings

How many words are there in the English language that are labels for feelings? Write down a guess. Given a time limit (one minute, or other determined by students), the students write down as many feeling words as they can think of. They then collaborate with a partner, add to the list, and write down a total.

2. The Sounds of Feelings

Distribute the Feelings blackline and have students mark or highlight all the words on the list they brainstormed. Choose a feeling from the list that you would like to explore. Give the students time to think of instruments, sounds and expressive elements that would help them illustrate the feeling word.

3. Time to Rubric

Pass out The Feelings Rubric. The rubric lists what the students need to include in their project and what behaviors they are expected to perform.

The Dramatically Different Classroom • Christine Laitta & Mark Weakland
Kagan Publishing • 1 (800) WEE CO-OP • www.KaganOnline.com

4. Review

Review what metaphors and similes are. Use the Metaphors & Similes blackline for review.

5. Teacher Models a Poem

The teacher models a poem before the students begin. Encourage the students to think in terms of metaphor and simile, but not write solely in these terms. For example, their poem about anger could look and sound like this:

- cold steel
  (a hammer hits an anvil)
- hot (sound of steam)
- breaking glass (smash!)

6. Students Create

Divide students into groups. Groups choose one or more words (it could be a totally new word from the list), write a poem and a soundscape for that poem.

7. Share

When groups are ready to share their feeling poems, decide on a performance order or have each group share with another group. Perform and record! Critique the work.

Enhancers

- Allow students to rework (on their own time) and rerecord a performance.
- Put tape or disk of recorded works in a learning or listening center.

Multiple Intelligences

- Verbal/Linguistic
- Bodily/Kinesthetic
- Musical/Rhythmic
- Interpersonal
- Intrapersonal

The Dramatically Different Classroom • Christine Laitta & Mark Weakland
Kagan Publishing • 1 (800) WEE CO-OP • www.KaganOnline.com

55

Feelings

Name_____

	depressed	jubilant
	desperate	mad
	disagreeable	mortified
	disgusted	obsessed
	disturbed	offended
	eager	peaceful
adventuresome	elated	perturbed
affectionate	exhilarated	proud
afraid	fearful	repelled
aggravated	fidgety	satisfied
agreeable	flustered	scared
anxious	fulfilled	seductive
ashamed	ghastly	skittish
awful	gleeful	splendid
bitter	grateful	timid
bored	great	uneasy
confused	guilty	unhappy
contented	hopeful	voluptuous
crushed	humiliated	weary
daring	impatient	winsome
dejected	inspired	wonderful

The Dramatically Different Classroom • Christine Laitta & Mark Weakland
Kagan Publishing • 1 (800) WEE CO-OP • www.KaganOnline.com

Metaphors & Similes

Name_____ Date_____

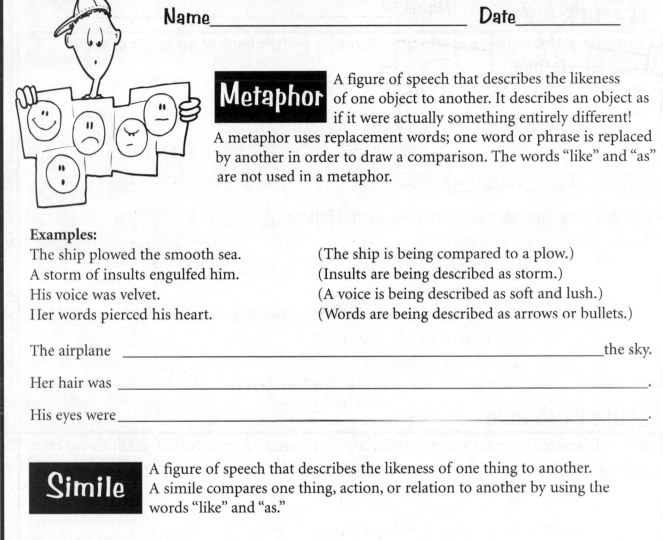

Metaphor

A figure of speech that describes the likeness of one object to another. It describes an object as if it were actually something entirely different! A metaphor uses replacement words; one word or phrase is replaced by another in order to draw a comparison. The words "like" and "as" are not used in a metaphor.

Examples:

The ship plowed the smooth sea.   (The ship is being compared to a plow.)

A storm of insults engulfed him.   (Insults are being described as storm.)

His voice was velvet.   (A voice is being described as soft and lush.)

Her words pierced his heart.   (Words are being described as arrows or bullets.)

The airplane _____the sky.

Her hair was _____.

His eyes were _____.

Simile

A figure of speech that describes the likeness of one thing to another. A simile compares one thing, action, or relation to another by using the words "like" and "as."

Examples:

Her voice was <u>as</u> loud <u>as</u> a fog horn.

He ran <u>like</u> a frightened turtle.

The moon was <u>as</u> bright <u>as</u> a searchlight.

The building towered above them <u>like</u> Godzilla.

She jumped like_____.

The night was as dark as _____.

His hands were as cold as _____.

The plane fell from the sky like a _____.

The Dramatically Different Classroom • Christine Laitta & Mark Weakland
Kagan Publishing • 1 (800) WEE CO-OP • www.KaganOnline.com

57

The Feelings Rubric

TEACHER RUBRIC

Students collaborated to create a multimedia performance of an original poem based on a feeling:

_____Yes _____ No

Rate quality of cooperation (highest to lowest)

5   4   3   2   1

Composition includes at least three of the following:

__ use of a metaphor

__ use of a simile

__ use of multiple sensory images

__ application of expressive elements such as tempo, timbre, and dynamics

__ application of sounds

__ expressive use of the voice

STUDENT RUBRIC

We collaborated to create a multimedia performance of an original poem based on a feeling :

_____Yes _____No

Rate quality of cooperation (highest to lowest)

5   4   3   2   1

Composition includes at least three of the following:

__use of a metaphor

__use of a simile

__use of multiple sensory images

__application of expressive elements such as tempo, timbre, and dynamics

__ application of sounds

__ expressive use of the voice

The Dramatically Different Classroom • Christine Laitta & Mark Weakland
Kagan Publishing • 1 (800) WEE CO-OP • www.KaganOnline.com

Tell Me a Story

Students tell a story using methods that engage the different senses. This activity gives students the opportunity to put themselves in the shoes of someone with a disability. It inspires creative problem solving, self-expression, and empathy. Avoid using computers and technology as a solution.

1. Discuss the Challenges of Being Challenged

Have the students brainstorm a list of free-time activities, then list the challenges that someone with a disability would have to overcome if he or she wanted to perform these activities. The teacher should point out additional physical aids students would need if they wanted to be part of the activities.

2. Select a Story

Students select a simple story to tell. The story must be well constructed without too many characters. A story with too many characters can be overwhelming.

3. Teacher Gives the Challenge

The teacher gives each student a specific audience to tell their story to. For example, one student may have to tell the story to a person who is blind.

4. Collect Teaching Aids

Encourage the students to research and experiment in order to find aids that will allow them to tell the story to someone with a disability.

5. Share, Critique, and Regroup

Have the students share their stories with the group and then discuss what worked best. Next put the students into several small groups. Have them tell a new story that the teacher has chosen or a story that a student read previously.

6. Share, Critique, and Discuss

Discuss what was different. Was it easier? What did they learn from the activity?

Stuff You Need

- A simple story that has a clear beginning, middle, and end
- Teaching aids that help the students tell a story to others who may be unable to see, hear, or speak

Stuff You Need to Know

People learn 15 percent of what they read; 20 percent of what they hear; 30 percent of what they see; 50 percent of what they read, hear, and see; 70 percent of what they read, hear, see, and experience; 90 percent of what they read, hear, see, experience, and practice. Now imagine that you are Helen Keller!

Enhancers

- Ask the group, "What if the person you are telling a story to doesn't speak your language? How can you then tell the story?"

Multiple Intelligences

- Verbal/Linguistic
- Visual/Spatial
- Bodily/Kinesthetic
- Interpersonal
- Intrapersonal
- Logical/Mathematical

The Dramatically Different Classroom • Christine Laitta & Mark Weakland
Kagan Publishing • 1 (800) WEE CO-OP • www.KaganOnline.com

59

Stories That Move Me

Without the aid of audio or vocal enhancement, students tell a story using only body movements. Through the use of representative movement, students simultaneously make stories come alive and stretch their body smarts.

Stuff You Need

- Examples of pantomime (video, books on technique, Charlie Chaplin films)
- A large clear space that will be easy to move around in

Stuff You Need to Know

This activity works best if you have already discussed and worked on body language. Before you begin you may want to take time to talk about how prehistoric peoples used body and hand movements to tell stories.

1. Power of Expressive Movement

Review examples of how movement can express situations, moods, relationships, and inner feelings.

2. Teacher Selects a Story

Choose a story that the group is familiar with and read it aloud.

3. List Important Story-Line Points

Discuss the major events of the story and list them in chronological order.

4. Select Movements

As a group, decide on actions that would be good substitutions for the narrative and the dialogue. Practice these movements.

The Dramatically Different Classroom • Christine Laitta & Mark Weakland
Kagan Publishing • 1 (800) WEE CO-OP • www.KaganOnline.com

5. Practice Movements

Choose the most effective and easy-to-understand movements to tell the story. Practice them.

6. Form Groups

Break the class into several smaller groups, making sure each group has enough people to tell the story.

7. Assign Stories

Assign each of the groups a new separate story. Encourage them to rehearse the movements and to interact with the other characters.

8. Share Movement Stories

Share the final products and be sure to point out the positive elements of each. Discuss why some were more effective. Redo the performances, incorporating the improvements.

Enhancers

• Have the students create their own stories.
• Create masks that represent characters or a specific emotion.
• Try acting out stories with a student playing more than one character.
• Pose the question: How will the student have to adapt to make it believable?
• Try acting out historical events.

Multiple Intelligences

• Verbal/Linguistic
• Visual/Spatial
• Bodily/Kinesthetic
• Interpersonal

The Dramatically Different Classroom • Christine Laitta & Mark Weakland
Kagan Publishing • 1 (800) WEE CO-OP • www.KaganOnline.com

61

The Story of My Life So Far

Students write truthful accounts of their lives' memorable moments and tie them together with their artistic expressions of choice. This activity is not merely a creative writing challenge. Because it incorporates the arts, it involves self-expression, pride in one's life accomplishments, and storytelling.

Stuff You Need

- Photos or drawings that complement a students story
- Examples of music, song writing, dance, pantomime, sculpture, drawing, and/or painting

Stuff You Need to Know

Color, sounds and smells are powerful triggers that remind us of life's special events.

1. Discuss Autobiographies

Discuss what an autobiography is and the different techniques a writer can use to reveal his or her life story.

2. List Possible Transitions

Make a list of all the different arts, such as dance, music, film making, and painting and then discuss the different techniques artists use to express themselves. Students select one or several artistic mediums to use as transitions between written autobiographical events.

3. Beginning, Middle and End

Students brainstorm the major events of their lives so far, then they write them down in chronological order.

The Dramatically Different Classroom • Christine Laitta & Mark Weakland
Kagan Publishing • 1 (800) WEE CO-OP • www.KaganOnline.com

Enhancers

• Videotape
• Share with family during open house

Multiple Intelligences

• Verbal/Linguistic
• Visual/Spatial
• Bodily/Kinesthetic
• Interpersonal
• Intrapersonal
• Musical/Rhythmic

4. Students Develop Transitions

Next, have them choose one or several artistic transitions that will take the audience from event to event. For example one student may sing a song about family or play a song from a CD. Another student may do a dance or create a picture. Each song, dance, or picture acts as a transition from one life segment to another.

5. Students Share Autobiographies

Students pair up and share their life stories, reading the events and presenting their transitions. This can also be done on an individual basis in front of the class.

6. Discuss and Share

Discuss the effectiveness of the artistic transitions. How did they make you feel? Were they difficult to choose? If so why? What affected you most as both the author and audience?

The Dramatically Different Classroom • Christine Laitta & Mark Weakland
Kagan Publishing • 1 (800) WEE CO-OP • www.KaganOnline.com

63

Express Yourself

Students write a poem based on an emotional event in their lives and share it with the class using expressive speech. The students gain a greater understanding of how to use expression and emotion when writing and presenting. This activity promotes self-confidence, self-expression, and creative writing.

Stuff You Need

- Examples of poetry
  (Try *The Road Less Traveled*)
- Audiotapes or videotapes of people doing poetry reading

Stuff You Need to Know

Give your students an insight into who you are by sharing your own life experiences in poetry form. Maybe you have a poem inside you about summer vacations, friendships, or the first car you bought. Sharing helps to establish trust and respect.

Enhancers

- Publish a book of poems.
- Publish a book for the school to buy.

Multiple Intelligences

- Verbal/Linguistic
- Interpersonal
- Intrapersonal

1. Create a Poetry Corner

Set aside a cozy space that creates a mood. Allow the students to decorate it as they see fit. (Lava lamps, paintings, pillows, and carpet squares.)

2. Share a Piece of Yourself

Before you ask the students to give a piece of themselves, give a bit of yourself by sharing a poem.

3. Inspire

Have the students watch videos of poetry readings. Bring in local poets and writers to share their creations.

4. Begin a Journal

Have the students carry a journal with them and jot down a poem when something in their lives inspires and moves them.

5. Share

Have the students select entries from their journal and share them with the class in a dramatic reading.

The Dramatically Different Classroom • Christine Laitta & Mark Weakland
Kagan Publishing • 1 (800) WEE CO-OP • www.KaganOnline.com

Sing, Sing a Song

Students and teachers sing songs, both to enhance the content of a lesson and as an alternate way to teach students with a speech/language disability. This activity promotes speech, diction, rhythm, memorization, building an ensemble, and self-confidence.

1. Choose a Song

When getting ready to plan a lesson, pause and think, "What song do I know that would enhance the speech language goals of this student?" For example, if your student is working on articulation, find a song that focuses on a particular consonant or vowel sound, such as *The Ascot Gavotte* from *My Fair Lady* or for younger children, *Sammy the Snake* from *Sesame Street*. If the child is working on expressive language, pick songs that stress communication or melody and pitch variance, such as *The Lonely Goatherd* from *The Sound of Music* or *It's a Hard Knock Life* from *Annie.*

2. File Your Songs

When you find a song that works well, jot it down and file it. Ask other professionals for suggestions and create a file together. This wealth of musical knowledge will be a wonderful resource.

3. Sing, Sing a Song

Use music in your class on a regular basis. Slow the song down and speed the song up. Review the song on a regular basis and note any improvements. In addition to its educational merits, it will be a treat for both you and your students.

Stuff You Need

- A file of favorite songs generated by the teacher and the students
- Songs that complement your lesson
- Song books (one per student)

Stuff You Need to Know

If you think this activity should be in the Taking a Break section, you're right! Singing is both a wonderful release and a powerful teaching tool, so we have included it in this section, too. Because singing uses both speech and language, it may serve as an alternative way to instruct students with a speech and/or language impairment. Sometimes a child can sing better than he or she can speak! There are many well-documented cases of actors and singers who stuttered as children, but could sing and recite entire pages of monologue flawlessly.

Enhancers

- Write your own songs to complement your lessons.
- Have the students write a song about a communication topic currently being studied. They can use existing melodies or write an original song.

Multiple Intelligences

- Verbal/Linguistic
- Interpersonal (singing with others)
- Intrapersonal
- Musical/Rhythmic

The Dramatically Different Classroom • Christine Laitta & Mark Weakland
Kagan Publishing • 1 (800) WEE CO-OP • www.KaganOnline.com

65

I Hear a Melody

In this activity, students sing simple songs in order to learn about pitch. This knowledge enables them to use more pitch variation as they read aloud, thereby making their reading more flowing, musical, and pleasing to the ear. Students discover that pitch is an important element of reading and should be used when reading all types of texts.

Stuff You Need

- Simple songs that the teacher can sing or sing along with
- Samples of pitch maps (see activity below)
- Songs on tape or CD (as needed)

Stuff You Need to Know

Simple songs serve as the basis for understanding how to vary pitch during oral reading. A strong melody has memorable and interesting changes in pitch. While a CD or tape can be used in this activity, it is best if the teacher is actually singing.

1. Sing a Song

Sing or play a well-known song that clearly demonstrates pitch rising and falling. In the following steps, we will use *Frère Jacques*.

Dormez vous

Dormez vous

2. Draw a Pitch Map

The teacher demonstrates pitch by drawing a pitch map of the first few lines of the chosen song. While singing or playing the song, point to the pitch map. Have the children listen and watch as the pitch rises and falls. Here is a pitch map of *Frère Jacques*:

Frère Jacques

Frère Jacques

3. Use Hand Motions

To further illustrate pitch, raise and lower your hands as the melody rises and falls. Have the students do the same.

4. Practice

Sing a number of different songs, use hand motions and map out the pitch on paper. Have the students practice using their hands and/or drawing pitch maps to show pitch variation.

The Dramatically Different Classroom • Christine Laitta & Mark Weakland
Kagan Publishing • 1 (800) WEE CO-OP • www.KaganOnline.com

5. Use Literature

Pick sentences and paragraphs from literature that would natural-ly rise and fall in pitch. Scary sto-ries and action stories are good ones to use. Demonstrate with a pitch map and hand movement. For example, the pitch would stay low for this phrase: "He could see the worms wriggling in the rotting carcass of the deer." Demonstrate how the pitch would gradually rise during the reading of this scene: "The pitcher released the ball. It sped toward the plate like a bullet. Casey tensed. He swung his bat! It was a home run!" Don't be afraid to exaggerate the pitch when you first start.

- Have the whole class do the hand movements while you read.
- Have half the students read and half do hand movements.
- Practice different types of pitch variation on the same sentences.
- Have one student "conduct" the pitch to the class with his or her hands. Allow him or her to experiment with using rising and falling pitch in different places.
- Ask: Which ways sound natural? Which don't?

6. Group

Group the students into pairs and give them a short paragraph from a mystery, suspense, or action story. Have them draw pitch maps over sentences that have natural pitch variation. One student reads with pitch variation and the other moves his or her hands.

7. Share

Students share their pitch maps. How do they compare? Students read their story para-graphs to one another. How do the readings compare?

Enhancers

- Create a human pitch map with students of varying sizes. As you sing a song, such as *Frère Jacques*, each student sings the corresponding note, rising onto their tiptoes or contracting toward the ground, depending upon the pitch. Try to keep the song moving.

Multiple Intelligences

- Musical/Rhythmic
- Bodily/Kinesthetic
- Verbal/Linguistic
- Interpersonal
- Intrapersonal

The Dramatically Different Classroom • Christine Laitta & Mark Weakland
Kagan Publishing • 1 (800) WEE CO-OP • www.KaganOnline.com

67

Rhythm and Reading

Students use small, handmade drums to tap out the rhythm of words, sentences, and paragraphs. This activity helps students to read more rhythmically, thereby improving the flow and speed of their reading. Students also discover that rhythm is an important element of reading and language.

Stuff You Need

• Small hand drums created from small boxes, oatmeal containers, margarine tubs, etc. (one per student)
• Short rhymes written on large strips of paper
• Poems by Shel Silverstein, Jack Prelutsky or others
• All types of printed text, such as books, magazines, cereal boxes, advertisements, short stories, etc.

Stuff You Need to Know

The goal of this activity is to have students impart emphasis to words as they read. This improves the speed and flow of their oral reading and makes the reading more interesting to the listener. It is best to start with words and then progress to short rhymes, longer rhymes, and finally non-rhyming text. In addition to adding a kinesthetic element, the drums are a strong motivator. Put them away when not practicing this skill and reinforce the idea that getting out the "reading drums" is a special thing to do.

1. Introduce the Drums

Students and the teacher bring in objects suitable for a drum. Decorate the drums. The teacher should then discuss the purpose of these drums as well as the rules for using them.

2. Warm Up

Before each session of drumming begins, give the students a minute or two to play on their drums. After this "free drum" session is over, the drums are only to be used for the rhythm and reading activity.

3. Start With Names

It is easiest to start with the rhythm of the students' names. The teacher can introduce the term "syllable" if he or she chooses, but this is not necessary. Gently go around the room and tap out the rhythm of each student's name. Have them do the same.

4. Move to Words

Next tap out the rhythm of three and four syllable words, such as buffalo, Indiana, elephant, Pennsylvania, etc. Discover which words have the same rhythm. Encourage students to go out and find long words to bring to class.

68

The Dramatically Different Classroom • Christine Laitta & Mark Weakland
Kagan Publishing • 1 (800) WEE CO-OP • www.KaganOnline.com

5. Put Words Together

Put two or more words together and tap out the rhythm. For example, buffalo-Indiana. Practice this often.

6. Find the Rhythm of Sentences

Pick short, well-known rhymes to tap, such as *Jack and Jill went up the hill...* or *Two, Four, Six, Eight, Who do we appreciate?* Practice slowly at first and then get faster. Put the rhymes on strips of paper. Practice different strips every day. Have the children break into groups and tap out different strips. Remind the students to play the drums so only their group can hear it.

7. Move to Poems

Tap out nursery rhymes with younger children. Always remember to link the word with the rhythms. In other words, make sure you are reading the text as well as tapping out the rhythms. Older elementary children will enjoy Shel Silverstein and Jack Prelutsky. Keep the poems short. Start out slowly, making sure everyone is watching the text, but don't go so slow that you lose the rhythm.

8. Use Other Types of Text

Copy short paragraphs from children's books, short stories, and novels. Try to find the rhythm in sentences that may not at first seem rhythmic. The students are gradually learning to impart emphasis to words, thereby making their reading more dramatic and flowing. If the class starts to get bogged down, pull out previously practiced and well-known phrases.

Enhancers

- Use this activity as a supplement to a regular reading lesson.
- Find age-and school-appropriate rap songs and tap out the rhythms on the drums.
- For a high school class, this activity can be an introduction to scanning Shakespeare. "Scanning" is marking the text with symbols above each word or syllable, symbols that denote soft and hard inflection. Shakespeare should be read with a rhythm, which is how Will wrote it, and this activity prepares the students to read Shakespeare aloud.

Multiple Intelligences

- Musical/Rhythmic
- Bodily/Kinesthetic
- Verbal/Linguistic
- Interpersonal

The Dramatically Different Classroom • Christine Laitta & Mark Weakland
Kagan Publishing • 1 (800) WEE CO-OP • www.KaganOnline.com

69

Elliptical Scenes

As they pair up and act out elliptical scenes, students learn how to interpret dialogue and use subtext in their writing and speaking. This activity promotes creative thinking, problem solving, ensemble, self-confidence, role playing, creative writing skills, speaking with inflection, and thinking outside of the box!

Stuff You Need

• Definitions:
Elliptical scenes–scenes that can be interpreted in many different ways.
Subtext–the complex of feelings and motives that is conceived of by an actor as underlying the actual words and actions of the character being portrayed, or the true meaning of what you are saying!
• A numbered handout with several different elliptical scenes on it (one per student)
• A clear space
• A pencil (one per student)
• Sample Elliptical Scenes blackline master

Stuff You Need to Know

As thinking and feeling people, most students respond to more than just the spoken word. They also respond to the way or the manner in which words are spoken. However, some students are not naturally able to interpret or respond when others speak to them. These students need to be directly instructed on how to interpret and respond to conversation.

1. Review the Definitions

Have the students write down the definitions of elliptical scenes and subtext. Discuss the definitions with them and model examples. You should also review the definitions of body language and voice inflection and then give examples of each.

2. Pair Up

Pair up students that have not worked together in the past. This encourages the students to discover similarities with each other. Have partners decide who will be #1 and who will be #2 in the scenes.

3. Pass Out Handouts

Hand out the blackline and have them circle their numbers down the page so they can easily follow along.

4. Answer the Questions

Explain that each student in the pair should be able to answer the following questions about his or her character.
• Who am I?
• What do I want?
• What is my relationship to my scene partner (are we strangers, relatives, friends, animals, inanimate objects, co-workers, thieves, etc.)?
• Where is this scene taking place?

Basic answers to these questions will suffice, but the more the students discuss and plan, the more complete and interesting their reading will be. The teacher decides whether the students discuss these questions and answers orally, in note form or in a full writing assignment.

The Dramatically Different Classroom • Christine Laitta & Mark Weakland
Kagan Publishing • 1 (800) WEE CO-OP • www.KaganOnline.com

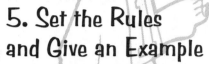

5. Set the Rules and Give an Example

After answering the questions, the pairs must create an entire story. At no time may they add any words to the scene. Here is an example of a scenario to an elliptical scene:

- The location is an airport.
- The relationship is that two old friends haven't seen each other since summer camp 10 years ago.
- The situation is they are both running to catch planes they can't miss.
- The challenge is they have mere seconds to express all of this. Have the students brainstorm ideas. They could do a secret camp handshake, hug or pass business cards to keep in touch. The possibilities are endless.

6. Preparation Time

Make sure the students have time to run through their scene at least once before they share it with the class. It should not feel over-rehearsed. Most of the prep time should go into the planning and character development.

7. Share and Discuss

Have each group share their scene and have the audience try to figure out what is happening. Ask the following questions:

- What is their relationship?
- Where is the scene taking place?
- Did they use their bodies to help tell the story? If so, what did they do?
- Did they use inflection in their voice?
- What did you like best?
- What else could they have done to make the scene even better?

Enhancers

- Write your own elliptical scene and perform it in at least two different ways.
- Videotape

Multiple Intelligences

- Verbal/Linguistic
- Visual/Spatial
- Bodily/Kinesthetic
- Interpersonal
- Intrapersonal
- Logical/Mathematical

Sample Elliptical Scenes

Scene One

#1 Hello!

#2 Hello!

#1 How are you?

#2 Fine. And you?

#1 It has been a long time!

#2 I was thinking the same thing!

#1 Will you be here long?

#2 I'd better be leaving now.

#1 I will be seeing you.

#2 Yeah, see you.

Scene Two

#1 What is that?

#2 I have never seen anything like that before!

#1 Let's get closer.

#2 Is that a good idea?

#1 It could be helpful…

#2 Oohh, my goodness!

#1 Oohh, my goodness!

Questions to Establish Subtext

1) Who am I?

2) What do I want?

3) What is my relationship to my scene partner (are we strangers, relatives, friends, animals, inanimate objects, co-workers, thieves, etc.)?

4) Where is this scene taking place?

The Dramatically Different Classroom • Christine Laitta & Mark Weakland
Kagan Publishing • 1 (800) WEE CO-OP • www.KaganOnline.com

Sample Elliptical Scenes

Scene Three

#1 Go!

#2 Go!

#1 I can't!

#2 Neither can I!

#1 Stop looking at me.

#2 I can't help it.

#1 All right, let's start again.

#2 OK, go!

Scene Four

#1 What was that?

#2 You know…

#1 It couldn't be!

#2 Nothing's impossible.

#1 Don't tell anyone!

#2 I am going to tell the world.

#1 I need to leave…

#2 No, stay!

#1 Will it happen again?

#2 Of course!

The Dramatically Different Classroom • Christine Laitta & Mark Weakland
Kagan Publishing • 1 (800) WEE CO-OP • www.KaganOnline.com

73

History of Storytelling

In this activity, students learn about the history of storytelling, how and why stories were passed on, and possibilities for preserving the art of storytelling for the future. Alternate ways of telling a story promotes creative thinking, self-expression, communication between students and adults, and respect of other cultures.

Stuff You Need

- Reference books with examples of hieroglyphics, mummies, fairy tales, Native American storytellers, and cave people
- Examples of journals, such as *The Diary of Anne Frank,* Louisa May Allcott's *Little Women* and *The Journals of Lewis and Clark*
- Oral histories of family members

Stuff You Need to Know

This activity will lend itself to many discussions. If a student knows someone in their family who is a storyteller, invite him or her to tell a story to the class. Be open to student ideas on story-telling.

1. Play Telephone

One of the oldest ways to tell a story is oral transmission or "word of mouth." Engage the students in a discussion of "word of mouth" storytelling by playing the following game. Sit the group in a circle and play the game Telephone. Telephone is played by whispering an idea into the ear of the person sitting next to you. Then that person repeats what they have heard into the next person's ear and so on until it reaches the original sender. Once the message travels around the circle, the creator of the message announces what they heard from the last person and compares it with the original word or phrases.

2. What Changed?

Discuss with the class why the phrase passed in Telephone may have changed. Compare this game to neighbors in Early America spreading news by word of mouth. Pose the questions, "Do we still rely on word of mouth today?" and "In what other ways do we transmit information and stories?" Don't forget the Internet.

3. Brainstorm

Have the students brainstorm a list of ideas of the ways people have shared and preserved their stories throughout time.

The Dramatically Different Classroom • Christine Laitta & Mark Weakland
Kagan Publishing • 1 (800) WEE CO-OP • www.KaganOnline.com

4. Make a Timeline

Have the students use their list to create a timeline of storytelling.

5. List Favorite Ideas

Have students list their favorite storytelling techniques (Folk songs, Oral stories, Dances, Symphonies, Operas, and Musical theater).

6. Challenge the Group

Challenge the group to figure out what they would do if the person you are telling the story to does not speak your language. How can you still preserve the story?

7. Create Options

Have the students create several different ways to preserve the same story. Share these ideas with another class. Ask the other class if they understood the story each time it was told.

Enhancers

• Have students preserve the history of their parents and grandparents in several different ways.
• Have your class tell stories to younger classes.

Multiple Intelligences

• Verbal/Linguistic
• Visual/Spatial
• Bodily/Kinesthetic
• Interpersonal
• Intrapersonal
• Musical/Rhythmic

The Dramatically Different Classroom • Christine Laitta & Mark Weakland
Kagan Publishing • 1 (800) WEE CO-OP • www.KaganOnline.com

75

Social Studies
(The Study of Social Stuff)

The Dramatically Different Classroom • Christine Laitta & Mark Weakland
Kagan Publishing • 1 (800) WEE CO-OP • www.KaganOnline.com

77

Little Schoolhouse on the Prairie

The students and teacher cover up the modern day conveniences of their classroom, thereby transforming it into a one-room schoolhouse. The students learn lessons from the pioneer era, and with the aid of the teacher they create a set of rules to make the experience as authentic as possible. This activity makes the past come alive.

Stuff You Need

- Tape
- Paper and/or boxes to cover computers, tape decks, TV, light switches, etc.
- A letter to the parents that explains the lesson and asks them to help by packing a simple lunch (no candy bars, sodas, prepackaged food, etc.)
- Slate and piece of chalk (one per child)
- One notebook and pencil (optional)

Stuff You Need to Know

This is a great follow-up to any lesson on Early America. Planning this lesson with the students is a major part of the lesson. Students and teacher should create this little schoolhouse together so when the day of the lesson comes, they understand the "rules" that they have developed.

Enhancers

- Try costumes.
- Invite different grades to attend your one-room schoolhouse.
- Turn out the lights and try candles, but don't set off the sprinklers.
- Videotape your experience, but try to disguise the camera so it won't intrude into your 19th century world.
- **Warning:** Recreating an outhouse in the hallway may not sit well with your principal.

Multiple Intelligences

- Verbal/Linguistic
- Visual/Spatial
- Interpersonal

1. Brainstorm

Brainstorm a list of changes that will take the classroom back to a little schoolhouse on the prairie. Refer to pictures and passages in books. Discuss what subjects would have been taught 120 years ago and which ones might not have existed. What pieces of equipment currently found in the classroom were not present 120 years ago?

2. Cover Up the New

Prepare the classroom by covering all modern-day conveniences and machines.

3. Teach

Hold classes in a traditional, 19th-century style. For example, have your students do their math problems on a slate. Do not use any handouts and read all lessons aloud. You may want to find examples of "readers" to give to the students. Caution: Do not use a hickory stick!

4. Time for Some Old-Fashioned Fun

During lunch and recess remind the students: no Game Boy, no football, etc. Do encourage tag, jump rope, hopscotch. "Spin the Horseshoe" may not be appropriate. Part of the assignment may be to research whether or not children had recess 120 years ago. If they did, try to find out what games might have been played.

5. Restore and Discuss

As you return the room to its original state, discuss what challenges the students had to overcome? How has our country changed?

The Dramatically Different Classroom • Christine Laitta & Mark Weakland
Kagan Publishing • 1 (800) WEE CO-OP • www.KaganOnline.com

The State I'm In

Students become a state and speak to the class as if they were the state itself. In this activity they research, interview and visit tourist information centers. This activity teaches students factual information on states and regions, and encourages them to be creative and dramatic.

1. Assign the States

Assign each student a state or draw states at random from a box.

2. Gather Information

Have the students gather information on the highlights of their state (similar to a travel brochure or promotional flyer). Information could be on natural resources, geographic features, interesting spots, industry, tourism, etc. Give the students time to really learn the information.

3. Rehearse

In small cooperative groups or pairs, students practice presenting the information. Encourage the students to really become their state. For example, if the student is from a Southern state, they should try speaking with a Southern drawl.

4. Travel to the States

Make the states available for visitation by taking the class to the cafeteria or other large open area for their "vacation sampler." Assign one group to be "tourists." Individuals from this group will travel to each state and gather information on each state. You can also physically group the states into regions.

5. Switch

Rotate the states and the tourists.

6. State Your Business

Recall and discuss facts about the states. Discuss what state you enjoyed the most and tell why.

Stuff You Need

- A wealth of information on the 50 states
- A map of the U.S. (for each student, used as a checklist)

Stuff You Need to Know

The students should draw on personal experience as well as research a number of different sources in order to discover the highlights of the state they choose. Because they will share their state information with their classmates, encourage them to discover "juicy" as well as pertinent facts.

Enhancers

- Dress like your state, speak in the dialect, use products from the area, etc.
- Invite other classes in to serve as the tourists.
- Apply this concept to countries of the world in a world cultures class.
- Videotape!

Multiple Intelligences

- Verbal/Linguistic
- Visual/Spatial
- Bodily/Kinesthetic
- Interpersonal
- Logical/Mathematical

The Dramatically Different Classroom • Christine Laitta & Mark Weakland
Kagan Publishing • 1 (800) WEE CO-OP • www.KaganOnline.com

79

Tableaux

Students form a living photo or tableau in order to re-create a historic moment. This activity promotes body language, self-confidence, and self-expression, encouraging the students to work together to creatively solve a problem. It is a great way for students to gain a deeper understanding of historical facts and events.

Stuff You Need

• A large clear space
• Pictures and/or factual information on a historical moment

Stuff You Need to Know

Before people could communicate with words, they used their bodies to convey language. The Greeks perfected this concept in the tableau, a frozen image that is used to tell a story. In ancient Greece the tableau may have been used to tell the news of the day. Some believe that the tableau was the beginning of modern-day theater. By calling on the students and inviting them to join the tableau, the teacher provides for classroom management. This activity works well with all age groups!

1. Brainstorm Historic Events

Brainstorm a list of historic events the class has been studying.

2. Select a Historic Event

Have the class vote on one of the events. This event is the basis for their tableau.

3. Discuss Main Ideas

Clear an area for the tableau. Identify the core action and characters in the event. The teacher should position students to represent the core action and characters to start the tableau.

The Dramatically Different Classroom • Christine Laitta & Mark Weakland
Kagan Publishing • 1 (800) WEE CO-OP • www.KaganOnline.com

4. Let the Picture Grow

Discuss with students the picture that is being created with their bodies. When a student has an idea or character that he or she wants to add, let that student join the picture. Watch it grow!

5. Think Outside the Box

Encourage students to think in terms of metaphors and similes. For example, the figure of Andrew Carnegie could be placed in a tableau with a book in his hand. This represents Mr. Carnegie's contributions to the public library system (see Enhancers).

6. Discuss and Critique

Discuss the completed tableau. What is being represented? What story is being told? Discuss other images you could have made. Could it have been a better image? Why or why not? Why are some images more powerful than others?

Enhancers

- Take a photo of the tableau and make your own history!
- Add props and costumes to make the scene really come alive.
- Supplement with music and puppetry.
- This lesson even works well with very young students. For example, a kindergarten class can learn about safety by taking an existing picture of a crossing guard at a bus stop and turning it into a tableau.
- This lesson can also involve higher level thinking!! Turn a lesson, a theme or a concept into a tableau. If the students have only one chance and one tableau to convey a complex concept or theme, they must be very creative! How can symbolism, metaphor and allegory be used to quickly convey complex ideas and events? How could the class make a tableau that represents democracy, checks and balances or capitalism?
- Agree on a series of tableau images that sequence into a story. Have the images melt and move from one tableau to the next.

Multiple Intelligences

- Verbal/Linguistic
- Visual/Spatial
- Bodily/Kinesthetic
- Logical/Mathematical
- Interpersonal

The Dramatically Different Classroom • Christine Laitta & Mark Weakland
Kagan Publishing • 1 (800) WEE CO-OP • www.KaganOnline.com

81

Step Inside a Painting

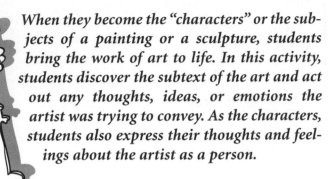

When they become the "characters" or the subjects of a painting or a sculpture, students bring the work of art to life. In this activity, students discover the subtext of the art and act out any thoughts, ideas, or emotions the artist was trying to convey. As the characters, students also express their thoughts and feelings about the artist as a person.

Stuff You Need

- Photos of a specific artist's work
- Photos of styles and movements in art
- Facts about the artist and if possible what the work meant to him/her
- The Sondheim musical *Sunday in the Park With George*
- Step Inside a Painting blackline master

Stuff You Need to Know

When students put themselves into a moment and experience it on a tangible level, art becomes real, moving and inspiring. This is the same idea found in the previous tableau activity, but this time the tableaux are used to unravel facts and subtext. The subject matter of the art may be human, but it could also be inanimate objects.

Enhancers

- Write a play about the life of an artist as seen through the eyes of a character or characters in her work.

Multiple Intelligences

- Verbal/Linguistic
- Visual/Spatial
- Bodily/Kinesthetic
- Interpersonal
- Intrapersonal

1. Choose a Piece of Art

The students are given pictures of a piece of art. The work can be art that they have previously studied or art that you would like them to research.

2. Form Groups

Use the number of characters in the picture or sculpture to help you decide how many students should be placed in a group. All groups can form the same piece of art or each group can be assigned a different work.

3. Plan It

Using the blackline master, have groups answer questions about the artist and the work, then plan their paintings and get into the minds of the characters and artist.

4. Cast the Characters

Have the groups cast the characters and then pose, mirroring what they see on the picture in front of them.

5. Bring it to Life

Allow groups of students to present their tableau to other groups. Have the visiting group ask the presenting group questions on the blackline about the artist and the work. When done, visiting groups present their works.

The Dramatically Different Classroom • Christine Laitta & Mark Weakland
Kagan Publishing • 1 (800) WEE CO-OP • www.KaganOnline.com

Step Inside a Painting

Artwork Title _____
_____

The Artist

Write a brief summary of the artists' life.

_____
_____
_____
_____
_____
_____

The Work

Where is the piece set?

_____
_____
_____

When was it painted?

_____
_____
_____

What does the work depict?

_____
_____
_____
_____

The Dramatically Different Classroom • Christine Laitta & Mark Weakland
Kagan Publishing • 1 (800) WEE CO-OP • www.KaganOnline.com

83

Step Inside a Painting

How do we feel about the piece?

- Person 1 _____

- Person 2 _____

- Person 3 _____

- Person 4 _____

- Person 5 _____

What is your plan to re-create the work?

_____
_____
_____
_____
_____
_____

Draw a picture of your plan to re-create the work.

The Dramatically Different Classroom • Christine Laitta & Mark Weakland
Kagan Publishing • 1 (800) WEE CO-OP • www.KaganOnline.com

Wax Museum

In this activity, individual students become historical figures and collectively the class becomes a wax museum, complete with on and off buttons! The wax museum allows students to learn biographical information, to review for quizzes and tests, and to develop the intrapersonal and bodily/kinesthetic intelligences.

1. Students Choose a Subject

Each student picks a famous figure from the historical era or event being studied. The teacher can assign multidimensional and complex figures, such as Leonardo da Vinci or Eleanor Roosevelt, to students who can handle them.

2. Students Research Their Subjects

Each student discovers as much about their figure as possible and prepares an oral presentation. The presentation can be in the form of a factual report, not necessarily written from the first person point of view, or in the form of a monologue.

3. Students Rehearse

The students should practice their presentations to the wall, in front of a mirror, with a partner, and in front of the class.

4. Design Your Costume

Create a wax museum by encouraging the students to create a costume, hairstyle, makeup, and/or the props they would use. For example, Babe Ruth might have dirt on his face, a bat in his hand, and a baseball cap on his head.

5. Get Ready

The class goes into the cafeteria or open area. Half the class becomes the "wax people" for the day and the other half are visitors. Students choose a pose reflecting their character. Put a sticker on their shoulder. This is the on/off switch.

6. Create the Museum

Groups of students visit each wax figure which they "turn on" by pressing the sticker labeled on/off. They listen to the presentation and move on to the next wax character. When all done, the visitors get their chance to become "wax people."

Stuff You Need

• Informational resources
• Stickers (one per student)

Stuff You Need to Know

Taking on the personality of another person sometimes frees up the shy and less self-confident student.

Enhancers

• Music, props, costumes, dialects.
• Programs, ticket taker, pedestals.
• Invite parents and/or invite other classes to visit the "Wax Museum."

Multiple Intelligences

• Verbal/Linguistic
• Visual/Spatial
• Bodily/Kinesthetic
• Intrapersonal

The Dramatically Different Classroom • Christine Laitta & Mark Weakland
Kagan Publishing • 1 (800) WEE CO-OP • www.KaganOnline.com

85

Talkin' History

Students review and test their social studies knowledge by appearing as guests on their very own talk show. As guests, they become whatever or whoever they are studying. This activity promotes role playing, quick thinking, and self-expression.

Stuff You Need

- Chairs placed in front of the room (one per guest)
- 4 x 6 inch index card with prepared questions dealing with material your class has studied
- Box or file to save question cards
- Microphone (if possible)

Stuff You Need to Know

The teacher is the host of the show, so you are in control. If the class is studying Pennsylvania, your students become Pennsylvania. The students' questions will reflect the students' preparation and insight. Have fun with this!
For example, the teacher/host asks:
"So Pennsylvania, where is your capital?"
Studio audience/class asks:
"What exactly does Pennsylvania mean?"
The students answer as the state:
"My capital is a town named Harrisburg and my name means 'Penn's Woods,' named after William Penn."

1. Create the Questions

After telling the students what guest (topic) will be appearing on the talk show, have them generate questions to ask the guest. In final form, these can be written on index cards or precut 4 x 6 inch pieces of paper.

Sample questions:
"Mr. Lincoln, what was the most difficult part of your presidency?"
"Is it true, Mr. Washington, that you never actually fought in Valley Forge?"
"Mr. Edison, what do you consider to be your biggest success?"

2. Review and Rehearse

Review the questions the class has prepared. Have the students pair up and practice answering them. Remind the students the better they know the information, the better they will be as guests.

The Dramatically Different Classroom • Christine Laitta & Mark Weakland
Kagan Publishing • 1 (800) WEE CO-OP • www.KaganOnline.com

Enhancers

• Pick five people for each guest and rotate them in and out of the guest seat.
• Film as video.
• During filming of the show, save room for commercial breaks. For example, "this show is being brought to you by the Union Pacific Railroad," or "Mrs. Smith's 6th Grade Class, dedicated to bringing the past to life."
• During the commercial break, students could take a spelling test or a bathroom break.
• Challenge kids to become "experts." After finding additional info on the era, ideas or characters, they can appear on the show as an expert or a professor of history.

3. Select Your Guests

Pick some students to be guests. If you are studying one subject, such as Pennsylvania, pick multiple guests to be the same subject and let them agree on the answer. They can answer in one voice or take turns sharing information. Some subject matter lends itself to many different guests. For example, if you are studying the Declaration of Independence, you could have four guests: Ben Franklin, John Hancock, Thomas Jefferson, and John Adams.

4. Establish Your Audience

The rest of the class will be the studio audience. You may want to provide the studio audience with questions to ask the guests. Make it fun by taking on a personality. "Welcome to Back Talk, brought to you by room 201. Today's guest is..." Applaud your guest.

5. Switch

Switch the panel and the guests.

Multiple Intelligences

• Verbal/Linguistic
• Visual/Spatial
• Bodily/Kinesthetic
• Logical/Mathematical
• Interpersonal
• Intrapersonal

The Dramatically Different Classroom • Christine Laitta & Mark Weakland
Kagan Publishing • 1 (800) WEE CO-OP • www.KaganOnline.com

87

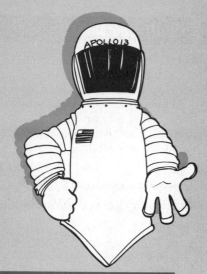

Voices From the Past

Students write a monologue based on a historical event or character and present it to the class or a partner. During their monologue, students are encouraged to "get inside the character's head and heart." Writing and performing a monologue gives students a chance to use their creative writing skills, allows for self-expression, and appeals to students' intrapersonal intelligence.

Stuff You Need

• Video clips of monologues
• Written examples of monologues

Stuff You Need to Know

The student should be very clear about the motivations of the character and/or the historical setting or fictional setting that the character lived in. The monologue should be a synthesis of emotions, motivations and facts.

Enhancers

• Costumes, dialects, props.
• Use a rubric to critique the class. How did the monologues compare, how did they differ?

Multiple Intelligences

• Verbal/Linguistic
• Visual/Spatial
• Bodily/Kinesthetic
• Interpersonal
• Logical/Mathematical
• Intrapersonal

1. Read and Discuss Monologues

Read and discuss written examples of monologues. Show video clips of characters engaged in a monologue. Here are some ideas:
Gettysburg (the movie)
1776 (the musical)
Apollo 13 (the movie)
Eyes on the Prize (on video)
Eight Men Out (the movie)
Evita (the musical)

2. Students Choose Their Subject

Students will choose the character that they want to become. Set guidelines for the length of the monologue. Give students ample time to write their monologues.

3. Students Memorize the Piece

Monologues are much more effective if memorized (or almost memorized). Encourage the students to memorize as much as possible and use note cards for prompting purposes.

4. Rehearse and Share

Students practice and then present their monologues to a partner, team, or to the entire class.

The Dramatically Different Classroom • Christine Laitta & Mark Weakland
Kagan Publishing • 1 (800) WEE CO-OP • www.KaganOnline.com

The Flip Side:
Seeing the Other Side of History

Given a specific event or era in history, pairs of students become opposing historical figures and dramatically comment on history as they see it. An example of this would be General George A. Custer and Chief Sitting Bull discussing the Battle of Little Big Horn or the doctrine of Manifest Destiny. The combination of in-depth historical research and innovative dramatics creates a chance for students to use their verbal/linguistic, bodily/kinesthetic, interpersonal and intrapersonal intelligences, and to realize that "truth" often has two sides!

Stuff You Need

- Video clips and written examples of dialogues between two people, historical figures if possible
- Examples of opposite figures, such as Galileo and members of the Church or Lyndon Johnson and Kent State students

Stuff You Need to Know

Be aware of and remind your students that this activity is not an exercise in fiction writing. Points of view must be defined (as much as possible) by what is within the historical record and must be defensible. At the same time, this activity is not dry science. Encourage the students to try to "get inside the head" of the person they are portraying.

1. Know Your History

Research and discuss a particular time in history and the people that played an important role in the events of the time. Decide if there are two figures on opposite sides that can be used for this activity.

2. Set the Stage

Pick two different characters and assign them to various pairs of students. Have pairs write a script or orally practice commentary on the same historical event.

3. Allow History to Unroll

Have the pairs of students practice their monologues or discussions. Then have them present to other pairs of students. Encourage discussion. How were the exchanges the same, how were they different?

4. Group Discussion

Discuss with the class whether history changes depending upon who is telling the story. Pose the questions, "Is it possible for both figures to be right?" and "If figures are right, what does this tell us about history and about truth?".

Enhancers

- Costumes, dialects, props.
- Use a rubric to critique the class. How did the discussions compare, how did they differ?
- Explore the characters further by having them appear on a talk show.
- To bring it to an elementary level, consider the Constitutional Convention. Some students could take on the role of delegates from the South, while others could take on the role of delegates from the North.

Multiple Intelligences

- Verbal/Linguistic
- Visual/Spatial
- Bodily/Kinesthetic
- Interpersonal
- Logical/Mathematical
- Intrapersonal

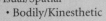

The Dramatically Different Classroom • Christine Laitta & Mark Weakland
Kagan Publishing • 1 (800) WEE CO-OP • www.KaganOnline.com

89

Our Town

Students relive a piece of history by physically changing their classroom, their behavior, and their outward appearance. In this activity, students go a step beyond observation. They actually create and relive the experience themselves. This activity makes the abstract concrete, promoting ensemble, self-expression, and creative problem solving.

Stuff You Need

- A letter home detailing what will take place and the needs of each child
- A room big enough for booths or desks and good flow of movement

Stuff You Need to Know

The students need to have an understanding of the time and people that they will be re-creating. Therefore, this is a great follow-up lesson to almost any social studies theme, such as Native Americans, Colonial America or South American cultures. You can also use this as a follow-up to a field trip where the students are observers, such as a museum or a battlefield. Planning this lesson with the students is a major part of the lesson. Create the world together by discussing the roles that people played in their community and how they affected the community as a whole.

1. Teacher Assigns Jobs

After reviewing the historic era that your class has studied, assign each student a role in the community you will create such as chief, mayor, candle maker, etc.

2. Students Create Their Characters

Students research their assigned roles by searching the Web, watching documentaries, talking to historians, writing for information, and rereading their textbooks. The students will research the types of clothing people wore for the work they did. Costumes may be representational. Students should bring in props that represent tools.

3. Students Write Speeches

Students prepare a presentation of who they are and what they do.

4. More Character Development

While appearing as their character, students engage in conversation with visitors. This is not regurgitating a prepared monologue. For example, a tribal chieftain who protects her tribe would talk about the history of her people and what means she uses to protect the land. She would be outfitted in appropriate clothing and may be "making" weapons as she talked.

The Dramatically Different Classroom • Christine Laitta & Mark Weakland
Kagan Publishing • 1 (800) WEE CO-OP • www.KaganOnline.com

5. Transform the Classroom

Rehearse the creation of this historical world by arranging the desks in your classroom to reflect the layout of "our town." Students can practice visiting and talking with the other people in their town.

6. Expand Your World

Transfer your world to a bigger space, such as a cafeteria, so the students have room to demonstrate to other classes how they work and live.

7. Recap and Discuss

Before or after you take down your town, you should discuss how the town may have been destroyed in a historical context. Follow-up questions could include:

• What did you learn?
• What did others learn?
• How did others interact with you?
• How were the visitors affected?

Enhancers

• Videotape.
• Add prerecorded sound effects to your town, such as horse-drawn carriages on a cobble stone street or wild animal noises.

Multiple Intelligences

• Verbal/Linguistic
• Visual/Spatial
• Bodily/Kinesthetic
• Interpersonal
• Logical/Mathematical
• Intrapersonal

The Dramatically Different Classroom • Christine Laitta & Mark Weakland
Kagan Publishing • 1 (800) WEE CO-OP • www.KaganOnline.com

91

Eating 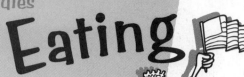 Goober Peas

The teacher uses music to enhance a U.S. history lesson. This activity provides a welcome break and often piques the interest of the the "hard to reach" student.

Stuff You Need

• List of possible music resources
• Tape recorder, turntable (remember these?), CD player, etc.

Stuff You Need to Know

Music can be a powerful force because it carries an emotional message as well as an educational one. Some songs, like *Fifty Nifty United States* carry factual information. Others, such as Jimmy Hendrix's *National Anthem* raise more questions than answers. Use songs to supplement a lesson or to teach the meat of the lesson.

Enhancers

• Consult with the music educator in your building to come up with more ideas.
• Create a master tape with the help of other teachers (including the music teacher) in your building. Share the knowledge and the music.
• Write your own song or have the students write a song to supplement the lesson.

Multiple Intelligences

• Verbal/Linguistic
• Bodily/Kinesthetic
• Intrapersonal
• Musical/ Rhythmic

1. Create Your "Hit List"

Create a list of songs and song books that can be used to supplement a social studies lesson. Here is a little list to get you started:

• *Fifty Nifty United States* by Ray Charles.
• *Goober Peas:* traditional, popular song with an ironic message sung during Civil War times.
• *Follow the Drinking Gourd:* traditional spiritual with symbolic meaning.
• *Capital Rap* by Rockapella. This teaches factual information.
• *Songs of the Civil War:* ed. Irwin Siber, Columbia University Press, NY, 1960.
• *Swing Low, Sweet Chariot:* spirituals sung by Marian Anderson.
• *Ohio* by Crosby, Stills, Nash and Young (U.S. History, 1960s).
• *National Anthem* by Jimmy Hendrix. What issues prevalent in the 1960s does this song touch on?
• *What's Goin On?* by Marvin Gaye.

• *The Great Dust Bowl* by Woody Guthrie.
• *Living for the City* by Stevie Wonder, a song that comments on race relations and the economic condition of African Americans.
• *Wild, Wild West* by Ziggy Marley.
• *Keepers of the Dream:* authentic flute solos and chants of the Lakota tribe performed by Tokeya Inajin (Kevin Locke).

Ask your students if there are any current songs that would add to the lesson.

2. Sing, Dance and Get Funky

With the power of your own vocal chords or with the assistance of a tape or CD player, you can play and sing the songs with the class. Move your bodies to the music!

3. Create a Listening Center

Put the songs on a tape at a listening center. Make sure you have a bunch of headphones!

The Dramatically Different Classroom • Christine Laitta & Mark Weakland
Kagan Publishing • 1 (800) WEE CO-OP • www.KaganOnline.com

What If?

Students generate guesses about what their lives would be like if history had turned out differently. This activity encourages recall of factual information, creative thinking, and synthesizing ideas.

1. What If...

The teacher first models an example for the class. Pick specific events in the historical era that you are studying and reverse the outcome. What if JFK had never been shot? What if the South had won the Civil War or Germany World War II?

2. Students Create Their Own Endings

Students pick an event, reverse it and elaborate by writing a report or in a journal. A more advanced step would be to write down two or three possible outcomes.

3. New News

Students work in cooperative groups of two to three in order to create a news broadcast that reports events happening in their alternate version of history. This can be done over the course of two or three days as time allows or at a special time of the day.

Stuff You Need

• Reference books and materials

Stuff You Need to Know

The students must have a clear understanding of what events shaped our country before they can conceive of an alternate history.

Enhancers

• Make a radio broadcast by recording the news broadcast on cassette and then playing it on a boom box.
• Create a small newsroom set, and videotape the newscast. Then view the skits at a later date.
• For older students, have them watch the nightly news in order to present a *Twilight Zone* version of the news events the next day.

Multiple Intelligences

• Verbal/Linguistic
• Interpersonal
• Logical/Mathematical

The Dramatically Different Classroom • Christine Laitta & Mark Weakland
Kagan Publishing • 1 (800) WEE CO-OP • www.KaganOnline.com

93

Beginning, No Middle, the End

Students work in pairs to "fill in the middle" of a historic event or era. This activity works well as a review for a test or quiz. It can also be used to assess student knowledge without a formal written test or quiz.

Stuff You Need

• Historical events that bracket a time in history. Two examples:
Beginning: "Abe Lincoln gives Gettysburg Address."
Ending: "Abe Lincoln shot at Ford's Theater."
Beginning: "The Pilgrims land at Plymouth."
Ending: "Squanto and Pilgrims sit down to a tasty dinner."
• Beginning, No Middle, the End blackline master

Stuff You Need to Know

This is a summarization activity that quickly develops communication and sequencing skills. The events that are used in the activity can be generated by the teacher, the students, pulled from a book or from a history text.

Enhancers

• Once the students are comfortable with this activity, you can have the students generate the beginning and ending events on their own.

Multiple Intelligences

• Verbal/Linguistic
• Interpersonal
• Logical/Mathematical

1. Pair Up and Pass Out

The teacher pairs up the students and gives each pair the same beginning and end of a historical event.

2. Students Research

Let the students use any resource to find the missing events. Remind the students to stick to the main events (leaving out that Mr. Lincoln, after reading the Gettysburg Address, walked off the stage, scratched his head, and took a nap).

3. Students Share

The students write down the middle events on their blackline and then present and compare their sequence of events with another pair. Allow the students to compare their sequence with at least two other pairs. Allow the student pairs to present their sequence in a variety of ways, such as simple oral reading, dramatic staged reading, script form, or a dramatic skit.

4. Discuss and Critique

Discuss with the class. Is there anything they left out? Did they choose significant events?

5. Repeat, Repeat

Allow the pairs to remain as is or create new pairs of students. Repeat the activity with another set of historical beginning and ending events.

The Dramatically Different Classroom • Christine Laitta & Mark Weakland
Kagan Publishing • 1 (800) WEE CO-OP • www.KaganOnline.com

Beginning,
No Middle, the End

Beginning Event _____
_____
_____
_____
_____

Middle Events _____
_____
_____
_____
_____
_____
_____
_____
_____
_____
_____

Ending Event _____
_____
_____
_____
_____
_____

The Dramatically Different Classroom • Christine Laitta & Mark Weakland
Kagan Publishing • 1 (800) WEE CO-OP • www.KaganOnline.com

95

The Oregon Trail Comes Alive

Teacher and students re-create and relive the Oregon Trail. Students research, plan and discuss the challenges that settlers were forced to meet and develop a simulation based on the facts. This activity can be adapted into a whole class activity that involves math, social studies, teamwork and problem solving. On a small scale, this activity can take place in the gym. On a larger scale, it should take place outside.

Stuff You Need

• Factual information on the lives of the settlers
• Large open field
• A list of obstacles and problems the settlers faced

Stuff You Need to Know

The Oregon Trail is a popular computer game.

1. Plan Your Trip

Before you set up Living Oregon Trail, the students should research what states they will travel through and what geographical obstacles they will encounter.

2. Students Create the Boundaries

Next, the students create the state "markers" and brainstorm how to build the physical obstacles. For example, large traffic cones or barrels could represent the Rocky Mountains or the Missouri River. They should also create problem cards that tell what problems the settlers encountered, such as physical ailments and lack of food. The teacher should have a supplemental list of problems.

3. Students Pack

The students brainstorm a list of all the things they need to take on the trip. The teacher should provide a list of items that the settlers must take, such as guns, bullets, flour, a tent, etc. The students compare their list with the teachers and decide what extra things they will take, keeping in mind weight and space considerations.

4. Students Create Their Characters

Each student should come up with a personal character. Here are some questions that help students create their characters:
• How old am I?
• What is my trade?
• Do I have any health problems?
• Why am I traveling?
• What is my name?
• What formal education have I had?
• Am I traveling alone or with my family?

The Dramatically Different Classroom • Christine Laitta & Mark Weakland
Kagan Publishing • 1 (800) WEE CO-OP • www.KaganOnline.com

5. Mark Off the States

The teacher and students go outside and mark off the trail and set up the geographical barriers.

6. Students Create Their Wagon Train

The students form a wagon train consisting of three to six students and give it a name. They should stay linked at all times by either touching shoulders or linking arms. The wagon trains line up and the teacher tells them to start their journey.

7. Teacher Poses Problems

As the wagon trains travel, the teacher calls each wagon train's name at different times and poses a problem to them. For example, the teacher says, "Weakland Wagon Train, your wagon has a broken wheel" and "Laitta Wagon Train, two of your members were bitten by a venomous snake." The groups then solve their problems by using their supplies and/or their knowledge of the area, the people and their customs. Students should discuss with the teacher how and why they overcame the problem before the teacher tells them to continue on their journey.

8. Travel On

Each wagon train continues until it reaches its goal.

9. Discuss and Critique

Discuss the experience. Did each wagon train work as an ensemble? What was the most difficult challenge? What supplies were most helpful and why?

Enhancers

- Could you adapt this activity for Magellan, Columbus, or immigrants to America?
- Incorporate props, scripts, etc.
- You can take this game and adapt it for a whole class activity that involves math, social studies, teamwork, and creative problem solving.
- Have a campfire and sing songs.
- Coordinate with your home economics class to create authentic campfire food.

Multiple Intelligences

- Verbal/Linguistic
- Visual/Spatial
- Interpersonal
- Intrapersonal
- Logical/Mathematical
- Bodily/Kinesthetic

The Dramatically Different Classroom • Christine Laitta & Mark Weakland
Kagan Publishing • 1 (800) WEE CO-OP • www.KaganOnline.com

97

World Music

Students and teacher create a library of world music that the teacher uses to enhance a world history or world cultures lesson. This activity provides a break in the normal routine, becomes an unusual addition to a lesson, and appeals to students' musical intelligence.

Stuff You Need

- List of possible music resources
- Tape recorder, eight-track tape player (we know you have one!), CD player, etc.

Stuff You Need to Know

Music is an endless teaching tool.

Enhancers

- With the help of your school's music teacher and classroom instruments, try to re-create the flavor of the piece that your students have heard.
- Students can create their own versions of world music and record them for the library.

Multiple Intelligences

- Verbal/Linguistic
- Musical/Rhythmic

1. Music for the Mind

Create a list of songs and song books that can be used to supplement a social studies lesson. Here is a list to get you started:

Europe: If you are studying the Renaissance, try music by the Baltimore Consort, such as *Dance of the Renaissance* or *Banks of the Helicon*.

Africa: Peter Gabriel's WOMAD organization has lots of good traditional music. For current music, try artists such as: Ray Lema, King Sunny Ade or Miriam Makeba.

Latin America: Try the artists Viento de los Andes or Los Folklorista for traditional music and Tito Puente or Ruben Blades for contemporary music. See what you can come up with!

2. Begin Your Class With Music

Introduce the lesson with a song. It's a great way to immediately attract the attention of your students. You don't even need to discuss, other than to say that it is from the area of the world that you are studying.

3. Review and Discuss

Later in the week, play the song again and ask students to use the knowledge they have gained about the culture and to comment on the song.

- What kinds of instruments do you hear?
- Why are these particular instruments being used?
- What do the instruments tell you about the culture and the history?
- What are the lyrics about?
- What do the lyrics tell you about the culture and the history?

The Dramatically Different Classroom • Christine Laitta & Mark Weakland
Kagan Publishing • 1 (800) WEE CO-OP • www.KaganOnline.com

Create a Culture

Students create a culture in order to understand the elements and interactions that make up culture. As they create their own culture, students work collaboratively, tap into their wells of creativity, and ultimately learn what culture is all about.

1. Discuss Culture

The teacher starts the activity by discussing the elements of American culture and then becomes more specific by identifying and discussing the elements of other cultures that exist within the U.S., such as African-American, Native American, Vietnamese, Mexican, and German. Have students share what they know about the various cultures.

2. Students Create Elements of Culture

Next, the students create elements that are specific to their new culture. For example, they may come up with a culture of people who dance instead of having a verbal language, who believe that you cannot eat alone or eat anything that grows under the ground because that is where evil spirits live, and who dress in clothes made from corn stalks and always carry umbrellas.

3. Students Name Their Culture

The students choose a name for their culture that reflects the overall belief system. The name of our culture is The Umbrallites (Um-bra-lites).

4. Share

Have one group present their culture to the class or have groups of students present their culture to each other. Students dress, talk and behave like people in their created culture. While one group presents, the other observes the culture and takes notes about the elements that make up that culture. Finally, have students demonstrate something, such as a greeting, dance, or a common belief, that they have learned during the presentation.

5. Culture Critique

Discuss the following:
- Did students address all the elements that make up culture?
- Were they able to show how those elements interacted with one another?
- What elements were most difficult to create?
- Did the group have to compromise on any issues, and if so, what?

Stuff You Need

- Examples of cultures and materials, such as documentaries, that examine and discuss specific cultures
- Create a Culture blackline master

Stuff You Need to Know

Culture is based on the shared beliefs of a group of people living in a common area. It is passed down from generation to generation as well as created every day. Culture is made up of economic structures, religion/mythology, arts, social rules, and conventions, clothing and material possessions, food, family structures, etc.

Enhancers

- Divide the class in half. Each half of the class develops their own culture. Have the students "live out" their culture for a class period. Discuss how these cultures interact and coincide with one another.
- Make up a dance that tells a story about the culture.

Multiple Intelligences

- Verbal/Linguistic
- Visual/Spatial
- Interpersonal
- Intrapersonal
- Bodily/Kinesthetic
- Musical/Rhythmic

The Dramatically Different Classroom • Christine Laitta & Mark Weakland
Kagan Publishing • 1 (800) WEE CO-OP • www.KaganOnline.com

99

Create a Culture

Group Members_____ **Date**_____

1. What types of social rules will exist? For example, how many hours a week will people work and will there be rules about marriage or freedom of speech? List your social rules.

_____

_____

_____

_____

_____

_____

2. What will you use for money? How will people in your culture feel about money? For example, will they work all the time to earn money or will they feel money isn't that important?

_____

_____

_____

3. Will there be an official language? If so, what will it be?

_____

_____

4. What are the religious beliefs of your culture?

_____

_____

_____

_____

_____

_____

The Dramatically Different Classroom • Christine Laitta & Mark Weakland
Kagan Publishing • 1 (800) WEE CO-OP • www.KaganOnline.com

Create a Culture

5. Describe some of the foods that will be found in your culture.

_____

_____

_____

6. Draw a picture of what people in your culture will wear.

[ ]

7. What will the arts and sports look like in your culture? For example, American culture favors baseball while England favors soccer. Brazilians love samba music while the Spanish like flamenco.

_____

_____

_____

8. Anything else to say about your culture?

_____

_____

9. What is the name of your culture?

_____

The Dramatically Different Classroom • Christine Laitta & Mark Weakland
Kagan Publishing • 1 (800) WEE CO-OP • www.KaganOnline.com

101

Family Tree

Students discover the legacy of their family tree by research-ing, writing, and sharing their family's history. Suggestions for the "sharing section" include ethnic dances, crafts, songs, and/or games that represent an important part of their family history. These significant pieces of family history are then taught to the class. Family Tree gives students an opportunity for self-expression, enables them to discover things about themselves, and stresses the importance of pre-serving family history.

Stuff You Need

- Tape recorder
- Journal (one per child)
- Photos/letters from each student's family
- Examples of different ways families have preserved their history such as a quilt or family recipes.

Stuff You Need to Know

This activity is a great follow up to a "World Cultures" theme. It empow-ers students to discover who they are by allowing them to learn where they have come from and why they have ended up where they are. These discoveries are especially important in today's multicultural and ethnically diverse classrooms.

Enhancers

- Videotape it and start a family history library.

Multiple Intelligences

- Verbal/Linguistic
- Visual/Spatial
- Bodily/Kinesthetic
- Interpersonal

1. Preservation Techniques

Discover the techniques that people have used to preserve family history, from tapes-tries to tape recorders.

2. Discuss What Will Work Best

Discuss which techniques are most effective and why.

3. Assign Project

Explain to the students that they are to write their own "family tree" which will go back in time as far as possible.

4. Hunt and Gather

Give the students ample time to complete the task of gathering information. Remind them they can interview with a tape recorder, seek out written documents, use the Internet, and pull from their own knowledge.

5. Introduce the Artistic Enhancement

Remind students that their written "family tree" will be based on and enhanced by a creative art. For example, it could be a traditional dance the family did, a song that they sang, and/or a game that they passed down for generations because it holds a special family meaning.

6. Share the Complete Project

In class, in groups or in pairs, students read aloud the written history, share the family art, and then teach that song, dance, or game to the class. Students are now passing on their families' traditions!

7. Applaud and Critique

Discuss what worked best in each presentation.

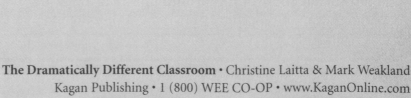

The Dramatically Different Classroom • Christine Laitta & Mark Weakland
Kagan Publishing • 1 (800) WEE CO-OP • www.KaganOnline.com

The Republocratic Party

Students work in small groups to create their own political party, unified in its beliefs. They then recruit others for their party. This activity promotes ensemble, compromise, problem solving, and knowledge of American government.

1. Identify the Platform Components

The teacher poses three major topics on which the group must find common ground, such as the environment, education, and health-care. The students then create a platform or a statement of beliefs, for example "caring for the environment is important to our country's future."

2. Group Students

Forming groups of four to six students, the teacher reminds them that they will be asked questions about their party from the audience. The audience is made up of the remaining classmates.

3. Create Platforms

Students make a list of the group's common beliefs. For example:
- "We believe that the environment should be used to make our economy strong."
- "We believe more land should be set aside for national parks."

4. Create a Party

After finalizing their platform, the students select a party name that reflects their beliefs. For example:
- "People for People" (The PFP). "We stand for volunteers of all ages, garbage-free cities, and free health-care clinics."

5. Share

The groups present their parties to the class through the use of stump speeches, posters and commercials. They try to recruit party members through a question and answer session with the audience.

6. Discuss and Discover

Have the class discover common beliefs and issues that the parties share.

Stuff You Need

- Poster board and poster making materials (enough for each group)
- Examples of campaign materials, i.e., brochures, posters, speeches, video clips

Stuff You Need to Know

Students need to have a strong understanding of America's political parties, including what they are, how they were formed, and what are some of their basic beliefs.

Enhancers

- Have a debate between two different parties.
- Videotape the debate.
- Have the party members appear on a talk show or newscast.

Multiple Intelligences

- Verbal/Linguistic
- Interpersonal
- Intrapersonal
- Visual/Spatial
- Logical/Mathematical

The Dramatically Different Classroom • Christine Laitta & Mark Weakland
Kagan Publishing • 1 (800) WEE CO-OP • www.KaganOnline.com

103

President for a Day

Students campaign for presidency, then perform various presidential duties. By becoming the president for a day, students are given an opportunity to experience some of the daily tasks of the president. Problems to be solved in this activity include how to plan a political campaign, make speeches, meet the press, pass laws, and sign treaties.

Stuff You Need

- Poster board for campaign posters
- Questions that the students generate on platform issues
- Examples of famous presidential speeches (sound bites) and campaign platforms
- Examples (from past to present) of laws, bills and and famous treaties

Stuff You Need to Know

Before undertaking this activity, students need a basic understanding of how a government official is elected to office. To tailor this activity to the needs of your specific lesson, make students a mayor, senator, speaker of the house, and/or town council member. Have students compile a series of questions on why they chose to go into government and what the job entails. Encourage students to contact their state officials by e-mail, letters, and/or a phone interview.

1. Revisit the Book

Review your lesson on government.

2. Pick a Platform

The students choose a platform that they will base their campaign on. For example, "As president I will find more money for arts education. I will also create free art centers for communities."

3. Plan a Strategy

Students develop a campaign strategy and answer these questions: How will I get the word out? Who should I target as my main audience? How will I get the funds? Students should do one or all of the following:

- Give a speech that tells why they should be elected for four more years.
- Make an ad (print, television or radio) that tells why they should be reelected.
- Address the nation and outline their new idea for one of the following: education, business, taxes, the arts, the environment and world policy.

The Dramatically Different Classroom • Christine Laitta & Mark Weakland
Kagan Publishing • 1 (800) WEE CO-OP • www.KaganOnline.com

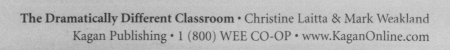

4. Set Deadlines

Give the students deadlines for each section. For example, "By next Tuesday you need to have your posters done and by Friday you will be ready to give speeches on your platforms."

5. Meet the Press

The students share their platforms with the class or in small groups. The class members who are not presenting their speeches that day become the "press." The press then pose questions to get a more in-depth understanding of what the candidate promises. The questions should be based on the age and ability level of the students.

6. Take Action

After students give their presentations, they now can:
- Draft laws, bills, and a treaty.
- Present an award to a heroic person.
- Present a treaty that promotes peace between two countries.
- Present a treaty that creates a trade agreement.
- Share ideas with those in the class taking on the roles of the House and Senate.
- Discuss the challenges the president faces.

Enhancers
- Videotape and broadcast.

Multiple Intelligences
- Verbal/Linguistic
- Visual/Spatial
- Bodily/Kinesthetic
- Interpersonal
- Logical/Mathematical
- Intrapersonal

The Dramatically Different Classroom • Christine Laitta & Mark Weakland
Kagan Publishing • 1 (800) WEE CO-OP • www.KaganOnline.com

105

Through the Eye of a Lens

Armed with a camera, students take pictures of a favorite building that serves the various needs of the community as well as a building that is not serving the community well. The goal is to revise the architecture of the second building in order to adapt it to the current needs of the community. Through this activity, students discover the importance of design and aesthetic appeal, think creatively, and use problem-solving skills to address a real-life situation. The history of the community and its architecture can also be incorporated into this lesson.

Stuff You Need

- One camera per child (fund-raisers or local businesses may help you attain disposable cameras
- Action Plan blackline master

Stuff You Need to Know

When designing a building, the architect takes into account the needs of the community and the aesthetic appeal and function of the building.

1. Get a Camera

Students can raise funds to purchase cameras, borrow a camera, or partner up with a fellow student who has a camera in order to complete the assignment. Ask a local store if they will donate services to this project. This can include developing or the cost of film.

2. Teacher Plans

The teacher then decides whether or not students will be responsible for taking the pictures on their own time or during class time.

3. Clarify Expectations

Provide students the Action Plan to assist them in completing this project. Review the steps involved in this project. Encourage the class to take the pictures from many different angles and heights.

The Dramatically Different Classroom • Christine Laitta & Mark Weakland
Kagan Publishing • 1 (800) WEE CO-OP • www.KaganOnline.com

4. Send Out the Students

Students go into the community and take pictures of buildings. For example, in one building a student may take pictures of people eating lunch in a lunch room, people working in offices, and children playing in and around the building. This building serves the community well. Next, students photograph a building that is not serving the needs of the community. This may be an abandoned office, an empty warehouse, or even a new skyscraper that is not community friendly.

5. Share

Students share their photographs in an oral presentation to the class or to a small group. Have students present their findings on how some buildings can be better adapted to fit the needs of the community. They also comment on the buildings which serve many different purposes in the community.

6. Propose Changes

Have students propose changes in the architecture of the building and tell why these changes are needed.

Enhancers

• Have a guest speaker come to the school and review and critique the projects.
• Take your ideas to an architectural firm.

Multiple Intelligences

• Verbal/Linguistic
• Visual/Spatial
• Bodily/Kinesthetic
• Logical/Mathematical
• Intrapersonal
• Interpersonal

The Dramatically Different Classroom • Christine Laitta & Mark Weakland
Kagan Publishing • 1 (800) WEE CO-OP • www.KaganOnline.com

107

Action Plan

Name_____ Date_____

- ☐ Walk through your neighborhood community. Observe the buildings and think about all the different ways they are used. What functions do they fulfill? What are they used for?

- ☐ Make a list of a few buildings in the community.
  Then comment on who uses them and for what purposes.

- ☐ Find an appealing building with multiple uses.

- ☐ Take a variety of pictures, illustrating the ways in which the building is used.

- ☐ Find a building in your community that is not being used to its best potential.

- ☐ Photograph the under-utilized building.

- ☐ Brainstorm and list ways that the building could be better adapted to fit the needs of the community.

- ☐ Present your pictures and findings to another student or group of students.

- ☐ Have another student or group of students brainstorm and list additional ways that your building could be changed or adapted to better serve the needs of your community.

- ☐ Present your pictures and findings to the class.

The Dramatically Different Classroom • Christine Laitta & Mark Weakland
Kagan Publishing • 1 (800) WEE CO-OP • www.KaganOnline.com

Mock Trials

Students take on the persona of a lawyer in order to research and defend their position on a law handed down from the teacher. As they develop a defense and present it in a mock trial, students must solve unusual problems, work as an ensemble, and gain a greater understanding of our legal system.

1. Teacher Presents a Rule

The teacher chooses a statement or a rule to bring to mock trial, for example:

• The world is flat.
• Driving faster than 40 miles per hour is illegal.

When first starting, make sure that students will be able to research and find facts to defend their points.

2. Group Students

Group students into legal teams and give them the task of creating their defense. Students can use all types of resources, such as encyclopedias, the Internet, the library, and their own background knowledge, in order to list reasons why the world is not flat or why someone should be allowed to drive faster than 40 miles per hour.

3. Judgment

The teacher acts as the judge and has students present their defense to him or her. Before making a ruling, the teacher should question the legal team and challenge them to think on their feet.

Stuff You Need

• Examples of court cases and trials, for example Brown vs. Board of Education, the Scopes Monkey Trial, the trial presented in the book, *To Kill a Mockingbird* and a current trial appropriate to the age of the students
• Resources for researching precedents

Stuff You Need to Know

Challenge the students to stick to their beliefs and prove their points. For example, if the teacher makes a rule of no talking in school, students would develop a defense based on the First Amendment and prove that the law is unconstitutional.

Enhancers

• A high school class may want to create a full-blown trial with two opposing lawyers, a judge, and a jury.
• Have students take opposite sides of an issue or law.

Multiple Intelligences

• Verbal/Linguistic
• Intrapersonal
• Interpersonal
• Logical/Mathematical
• Bodily/Kinesthetic

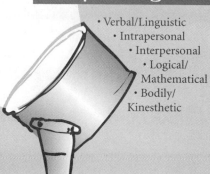

The Dramatically Different Classroom • Christine Laitta & Mark Weakland
Kagan Publishing • 1 (800) WEE CO-OP • www.KaganOnline.com

109

The History of Art

Students create an interactive board game that combines an art history lesson, a role-playing activity, and a review of a specific artist's work. During this activity, students, like the artists they are studying, practice self-expression, creativity, and problem solving, utilizing many of their intelligences.

Stuff You Need

- Examples of board games
- Pictures of the artist's work reduced to fit on cards that can be piled on the game board
- Examples of different game boards
- Names of artists printed on cards
- Dice or a student-created gadget that lets the players know how many spaces they will be moving.

Stuff You Need to Know

Encourage students to incorporate their tableau skills (see Social Studies Activity 3), and monologue skills (Social Studies Activity 7) into the creation of their game. Students need to have a strong knowledge of an artist's specific works prior to doing this activity. This activity can also be adapted for the study of Egyptian art, architectural styles and advancements, modern art, and much more.

1. Select the Theme

Students will agree on one of the following:
- A specific artist and his or her work.
- An architectural style and it's developments.
- An artistic movement or school of thought.

2. Design the Board

Students design and draw their own model of a game board. Encourage students to incorporate monologues and tableaux into the game.

3. Share

Have students share their concept with the class. Combine the "best" ideas from each student into a single concept.

4. Finalize Your Design

With the guidance of the teacher, students create a single game board. Discuss how it will be constructed. What materials will be used? What will the layout of the board look like?

The Dramatically Different Classroom · Christine Laitta & Mark Weakland
Kagan Publishing · 1 (800) WEE CO-OP · www.KaganOnline.com

5. Set the Rules

Students and the teacher decide upon the rules that the players must follow. Here are some examples:

- You will need at least two teams to play.
- Four players per team.
- You have one minute to create your tableaux and bring it to life.
- If you land on an artist card you can only talk about the artist in the first person.
- Your team can only ask yes or no questions to guess who you are. For example, "My name is van Gogh" is not allowed but, the student could say, "I painted a famous self-portrait in a Post-Impressionistic style."

6. Teacher Forms Groups

Group students in fours. Designate a specific area for each group to meet and work in.

7. Assign Specific Tasks

Students are given a specific task to complete. For example, one designs the game cards, one colors the board, one collects and cuts pictures, etc.

8. Draft Construction Documents

With the teacher's aid and guidance, students draft blueprints of the game board that show examples of how their section will be put together.

9. Dry Run

The students test the game as they build it to make sure the parts work together and form a complete package.

10. Put It Together

Have the students refer to the construction/design documents so that they can piece the project together.

11. Celebrate

When you have finished, have a party and play the new game.

Enhancers

- Eliminate steps to bring the activity down grade levels. For example, leave out the drafting and blueprints steps.
- Have students who are playing the parts of the artist draw or sculpt in the style of the artist they are portraying.

Multiple Intelligences

- Verbal/Linguistic
- Visual/Spatial
- Bodily/Kinesthetic
- Interpersonal
- Intrapersonal
- Logical/Mathematical

Mathematics
(The Stuff That Adds to Our Lives)

Alice's Restaurant

Stuff You Need

- Catalogs and magazines that contain a lot of pictures of food
- Poster board, scissors, and glue or glue sticks
- Markers and pens
- Real order slips or teacher-made
- Calculator
- Play money

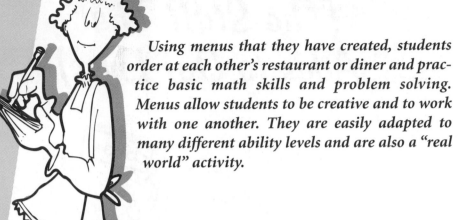

Using menus that they have created, students order at each other's restaurant or diner and practice basic math skills and problem solving. Menus allow students to be creative and to work with one another. They are easily adapted to many different ability levels and are also a "real world" activity.

Stuff You Need to Know

Many types of math skills and many ability levels can be built into this activity.

Enhancers

- Increase the number of items on the menu and change the prices to make for more difficult calculations.
- List the prices in francs, yen, British pounds, or some other foreign currency. Teach and practice monetary conversions while learning a bit about world cultures.
- Pose problem-solving questions to the owners: Can you take your family of four to eat at your restaurant for $35.00? What could that family buy? Would there be any change?
- If you live in a state that adds a tax to a restaurant bill, calculate and add the tax to get the total.
- Take the order's total and add a gratuity. What would be the total if you had to add a 10 percent tip? A 15 percent tip?
- Use the menus in this year's learning centers.
- Keep the menus and put them in next year's centers.

Multiple Intelligences

- Logical/Mathematical
- Verbal/Linguistic
- Bodily/Kinesthetic
- Interpersonal

1. Model a Menu

The teacher can model a menu of his or her own creation. Each menu should have the name of the dining establishment at the top and should include a wide variety of items and prices.

2. Students Create

Students can be allowed to work by themselves or with a partner. Give students ample time to think of a name for their restaurants, cut out food items for the menu, and then design the menu. Encourage them to be creative. Make sure they list prices with both dollars and cents, such as $4.95 or $12.55.

3. Gather in the Restaurant

After the menus have been created, students are grouped in fours. They then take turns ordering at the restaurant. Although one group orders and another group takes the order, all the students should know how much the total is and what their change will be.

The Dramatically Different Classroom • Christine Laitta & Mark Weakland
Kagan Publishing • 1 (800) WEE CO-OP • www.KaganOnline.com

Larger Than Life Math

This activity is based on the idea of a scavenger hunt. Students search for real-world examples of the math concepts being studied in class. Students connect mathematical concepts to the world around them.

1. Brainstorm Examples

After discussing examples in the text book, brainstorm a list of large, real-world examples of specific math concepts. For example, when asked to find parallel lines, students think of the two hallway walls or the banister rails going down the stairwells. The teacher may want to create a printed list based on the examples generated so that all students have something to get them started.

2. Send Students Out

Encourage students to take time after school to locate examples of the math concepts in their community. These examples can be described in writing, but it is much better if you can find a way to give each student or a group of students a disposable camera. Students take one good picture of the real-life math example and list the time, date and location of the find. At the end of the month, develop the roll of film and create a bulletin board.

Stuff You Need

- A few prepared real-world examples of the math concept being studied
- One camera per student or group of students (fund-raisers or local businesses may help you attain disposable cameras)

Stuff You Need to Know

This activity works best with geometric shapes and forms, such as parallel lines and rectangular prisms, but it can be applied to upper-level math concepts. For example, you may ask your class to find examples of large triangles, such as an escalator in a department store or the Duquesne Inclined Plane in downtown Pittsburgh, that would lend themselves to trigonometry problems and calculations.

Enhancers

- Use scavenger hunts in other subjects:
  Biology: Find an example of adaptive evolution, find a vascular plant, find an invertebrate.
  Chemistry: Find an example of oxidation (a rusty nail!), find an example of a polymer.
  Music: Find a song that uses a trumpet, find a song with sixteenth notes.

Multiple Intelligences

- Logical/Mathematical
- Verbal/Linguistic
- Bodily/Kinesthetic
- Interpersonal
- Visual/Spatial
- Naturalist

The Dramatically Different Classroom • Christine Laitta & Mark Weakland
Kagan Publishing • 1 (800) WEE CO-OP • www.KaganOnline.com

115

Mathematics
Activity 3

Vacation Stations

After students create places to visit, eat, and stay during a vacation, they calculate the cost of going on a vacation. In this activity, students use their logical/mathematical intelligence as they travel around the room.

Stuff You Need

- Magazines with pictures of vacation destinations, such as Yellowstone or Chicago
- Magazines with pictures of cars, pictures of houses, hotels or motels, and magazines with pictures of food or restaurants
- Poster board, scissors, glue, markers and pens
- Calculators
- Vacation Planner blackline master

Stuff You Need to Know

The students create four "vacation components," which are pictures of either a destination, transportation, hotel, or restaurant on the front of poster board and additional information on the back.

1. Create Vacation Components

Students can work alone or in pairs to create four vacation components:
- Destination poster board with a picture and title of a destination on the front and the total spending of one day at the destination on the back. For example, Sea World, $22.00 for an all-day pass.
- Car/van picture and name of the car on the front, miles per gallon on the back.
- Hotel picture and name on front, price of a one-night stay on back.
- Restaurant picture and name on front, price for one breakfast, one lunch, and one dinner on the back.

2. Teacher Creates Stations

The teacher gathers all the hotel, restaurant, and destination components, stacks them in three piles and then shuffles each pile. Then she picks one component from each of the piles. A stack of three components makes a vacation station. For example, the teacher may pick Disney World, the Five Star Motel, and the Family Diner.

3. Select Transportation

Next the teacher gives each group a car or van or students can pick one.

The Dramatically Different Classroom • Christine Laitta & Mark Weakland
Kagan Publishing • 1 (800) WEE CO-OP • www.KaganOnline.com

4. Put Out the Stations

Decide the following:

- How many stations will I put out?
- How many destinations will a student visit?
- Can the student spend more than one night at a destination?
- Do they have to consider gas mileage?

There are many other parameters that you may want to consider. However, you should start out simply. For example, students can pick three places to stay, they can stay one night only, and they will be buying only lunch and dinner.

5. Students Take a Vacation

Students work alone or in groups to design a vacation and then calculate the cost of going on vacation using the Vacation Planner blackline. They travel around the room, visiting their destinations and calculating the costs involved.

6. Share

Students share their final plans with one or two other groups.

Enhancers

- Take a vacation with a family of four.
- Take a vacation for under $200 dollars.
- Take a vacation and include the money you will need for gas.
- Calculate tolls and other expenses.
- Create vacation stations that will take you overseas or around the world. This is a perfect way to include older students and incorporate world cultures and social studies.

Multiple Intelligences

- Logical/Mathematical
- Verbal/Linguistic
- Bodily/Kinesthetic
- Interpersonal
- Intrapersonal

The Dramatically Different Classroom • Christine Laitta & Mark Weakland
Kagan Publishing • 1 (800) WEE CO-OP • www.KaganOnline.com

117

Vacation Planner

Group members_____ Date_____

What is the type of car or van you are driving?_____

How many miles per gallon does it get? _____

1. What is your first vacation destination? _____

    a. What is the cost of this destination?_____

    b. Where will you be staying?_____

    c. How many nights will you be staying? _____

    d. What is the total cost of lodging? _____

    e. Where will you be dining? _____

    f. What is your total food bill? _____

    g. What is your total cost for this destination? _____

    To find g add the following: $a + d + f$

2. What is your second vacation destination? _____

    a. What is the cost of this destination? _____

    b. Where will you be staying? _____

    c. How many nights will you be staying? _____

    d. What is the total cost of lodging? _____

    e. Where will you be dining? _____

    f. What is your total food bill? _____

    g. What is your total cost for this destination? _____

    To find g add the following: $a + d + f$

The Dramatically Different Classroom • Christine Laitta & Mark Weakland
Kagan Publishing • 1 (800) WEE CO-OP • www.KaganOnline.com

Vacation Planner

3. What is your third vacation destination? _____

    a. What is the cost of this destination? _____

    b. Where will you be staying? _____

    c. How many nights will you be staying? _____

    d. What is the total cost of lodging? _____

    e. Where will you be dining? _____

    f. What is your total food bill? _____

    g. What is your total cost for this destination? _____

    To find *g* add the following: $a + d + f$

4. What is your fourth vacation destination? _____

    a. What is the cost of this destination? _____

    b. Where will you be staying? _____

    c. How many nights will you be staying? _____

    d. What is the total cost of lodging? _____

    e. Where will you be dining? _____

    f. What is your total food bill? _____

    g. What is your total cost for this destination? _____

    To find *g* add the following: $a + d + f$

What is the total cost of your vacation? _____

    (Add all the letters g)

The Dramatically Different Classroom • Christine Laitta & Mark Weakland
Kagan Publishing • 1 (800) WEE CO-OP • www.KaganOnline.com

119

Scavenger Hunt

Students go on a scavenger hunt for math terms and concepts. This mathematical scavenger hunt promotes higher-level thinking, shows how concepts are related to the real world, and can be used to review for a quiz or test.

Stuff You Need

• Scavenger list based on the lesson or theme
• Rulers and scales if needed
• Polaroid camera (optional)
• Scavenger List blackline master

Stuff You Need to Know

Scavenger hunts can be easily adapted for a wide variety of subjects and student ability levels. These hunts get your students up on their feet and thinking creatively. They can be highly motivating because they involve real world examples. Make sure that you take time to discuss the physical and behavioral rules that must be followed during the hunt. You may also need to put certain areas off limits.

Enhancers

• Increase the opportunity for calculations. For example, find examples of fractions and then have students total them.
• Increase verbal skills. For example, find decimals and then read them.
• Offer a scavenger hunt for extra credit.
• Assign a scavenger hunt for homework. For example, find five examples of decimals.
• Adapt the activity to the metric system.

Multiple Intelligences

• Logical/Mathematical
• Verbal/Linguistic
• Bodily/Kinesthetic
• Interpersonal
• Visual/Spatial
• Naturalist

1. Set Up the Course

Find as many objects and/or clues as possible relating to the mathematical concept(s) being studied. This preparation acts as a management strategy; you have guided students' exploration and supplied them with appropriate items to bring back. (For older students, see Enhancers).

2. Create the List

Create the list based on the subject matter. You may want to provide the first couple of lists for students, but later they will be able to work in groups to create their own lists.
Here are two short examples:
Measurement
• Find an object 9 inches long
• Find a box and measure it
• Find an ear and measure it
• Find an object about 3 yards long
• Find a shoe larger than 10 inches long
• Find an object longer than 15 feet

End of the year review
• Find an example of a mixed number
• Find a rhomboid
• Find a decimal to the thousandths
• Find a mathematical symbol
• Find a fraction
• Find a rectangular prism

3. Begin the Hunt

Send students out in pairs or individually, depending on your preference.

4. Discuss and Share

Have the teams pair up and discuss and share what they found. Make sure that this does not turn into a competition where "the most objects found wins."

The Dramatically Different Classroom • Christine Laitta & Mark Weakland
Kagan Publishing • 1 (800) WEE CO-OP • www.KaganOnline.com

Scavenger List

Group Members_____

Measurement

☐ Find an object 9 inches long.   What is it? _____

☐ Find a book and measure it.   How long is it?_____

☐ Find an object 3 yards long.   What is it? _____

☐ Find something longer   What is it? _____
   than 15 feet.
                                      How long is it?_____

☐ Find something shorter   What is it? _____
   than 3 inches.
                                      How long is it?_____

Shapes

☐ Find a square.   What is it? _____

☐ Find a rectangular prism.   What is it? _____

☐ Find a sphere.   What is it? _____

☐ Find a circle.   What is it? _____

☐ Find a cube.   What is it? _____

☐ Find a cone.   What is it? _____

☐ Find a triangle.   What is it? _____

☐ Find a rectangle.   What is it? _____

Greatest Hits

Throughout the year students and the teacher create techniques, "tricks" or shortcuts, such as raps, rhymes, chants, acronyms, and mnemonics that help the class learn and recall math material. The class then creates a "Greatest Hits Album" which is used to review for quizzes and tests.

Stuff You Need

- Old album covers (four or five)
- A Polaroid camera
- Videotape and recorder
- Cassette tapes and recorder
- Recordable CDs, scanners, computer recording equipment

Stuff You Need to Know

In this activity, the teacher and students work together to create and use any tricks that help the class to learn and remember math material. These "tricks" and "shortcuts" are then gathered in a collection that should be easily accessible to the students. The way in which this collection is created depends upon the availability of technology and the age of your students.

1. Create Tricks

Throughout the year, teach your students to look for, create and use mnemonic devices, raps, acronyms, and other "shortcuts and tricks" that will help them succeed in math. Math books often give examples of shortcuts and most math teachers have a few tricks up their sleeves. Later, student may become adept at creating their own. Examples are given below:

- **Long division steps:**
  <u>M</u>other, <u>D</u>aughter, <u>S</u>ister,
  <u>B</u>rother, <u>R</u>over
  <u>M</u>ultiply, <u>D</u>ivide, <u>S</u>ubtract,
  <u>B</u>ring down, <u>R</u>emainder
- **Finding the fraction of a whole number:**
  Divide by the bottom, Multiply the Top! (chant many times)
  $\frac{3}{7}$ of 28 = 12

- **Placing a comma for place value:**
  One two three, cha cha, one, two, three, comma!
  (count from one's place to the thousandth's place)
- **Problem-solving strategy:**
  <u>U</u>gly <u>P</u>igs <u>S</u>nort <u>L</u>oudly
  <u>U</u>nderstand, <u>P</u>lan, <u>S</u>olve,
  <u>L</u>ook back

2. Gather Tricks

As you complete chapters, themes, sections or nine-week sessions and progress through the math curriculum, encourage students to gather up the tricks they find or create. The teacher can help in this process. You may want to collect them on file cards or in a file folder.

The Dramatically Different Classroom • Christine Laitta & Mark Weakland
Kagan Publishing • 1 (800) WEE CO-OP • www.KaganOnline.com

3. "Record" Your Greatest Hits

The best combination for any album is when the lyrics are included with the music. So try to have the tricks recorded on audio or videotape and have a companion written piece.

4. Art Work

Design album, CD, or tape covers.

5. Play the Hits

Review with the whole class or allow access to the hits so that the students can use them at any time, especially before tests and quizzes.

Advanced Mnemonic Devices

The following examples were e-mailed to us by Mr. Eric Lee, a lover of mnemonic devices who also happens to be a med-school student. He created the first mnemonic to help him remember the workings of the Epstein-Barr virus and associated diseases. The second one helped him to remember the names and locations of the hand bones. We have included these examples to provide inspiration and to demonstrate that learning "tricks" such as mnemonic devices are used at all levels of learning, from kindergarten to doctoral work!

#1 So, there's this place called Epstein's Bar. A bicycle is parked outside (which means cyclovir/gancyclovir are effective). There's also a bouncer at the door. In order to get in when you are underage, you have to bribe him with 3 CDs (CD3 receptor). He lets you in and as you walk in the door, you spit on the floor (shedding) and toss a ring into a tent by the door. (The tent always represented the nucleus. Some viruses were in there, some weren't; some used the ring, or plasmid, and some didn't.) You walk in and the place is kind of dark and smoky. In the back of the room you can see a bunch of college students necking; they all have flu like symptoms from mono. Many belong to the Theta Theta Theta fraternity (bunch of T cells). Some Africans are there and they're really sick with Burkitt's lymphoma. An Asian man walks up to you and sticks out his hand and says "Hi, I'm Harry Loo" with a strange lisp because he has hair all over his tongue (hairy leukoplakia). You worry he might be HIV+.

#2 To remember the actual names of the hand bones, you need the first syllable or so of each bone.

Here is the mnemonic:
"scared lunies try (a) pistol"
Here are the bones:
scaphoid, lunate, triquetrium, and pisiform
Here is the mnemonic:
"trap trap cap (and) ham"
Here are the bones:
trapezium, trapezoid, capitate, and hamate

Enhancers

- Use the Greatest Hits in a learning center.
- Save the Greatest Hits for next year's centers.
- Create a Greatest Hits album for other subjects, like spelling or social studies.
- Create Hits and encourage students to make their own for advanced subjects, such as chemistry and physics.

Multiple Intelligences

- Musical/Rhythmic
- Logical/Mathematical
- Verbal/Linguistic
- Interpersonal

The Dramatically Different Classroom • Christine Laitta & Mark Weakland
Kagan Publishing • 1 (800) WEE CO-OP • www.KaganOnline.com

123

Math Theatre

In order to make the abstract concrete, students and the teacher create and act out math concepts in short skits. Students can create puppets or develop their own characters. By creating a physical representation of a concept, students come to a deeper understanding of the math.

Stuff You Need

- A script that spells out the characters and what they want

Stuff You Need to Know

The teacher and students give human characteristics to math concepts, problems and/or symbols. It is helpful if the students have already been introduced to the concept that is going to be acted out.

Enhancers

- Videotape, share it with other classes, use it as a review or a learning center.
- Make it an extra credit activity for older students teaching younger students.
- Perform it live for other classes
- Take it on tour!

Multiple Intelligences

- Logical/Mathematical
- Verbal/Linguistic
- Bodily/Kinesthetic
- Interpersonal

1. Review

The teacher reviews the lesson and prepares students to present it in a new way.

2. Set the Scene

Students decide on a scenario for their skit. They choose the characters based on their mathematical properties.

3. Write the Script

In small groups, students brainstorm situations and write dialogue for their mathematical characters. Here is one idea:
"Shoot Out at the Mathematics Corral"
Addy (addition)–She helped bring the family together "All right, both of you groups get together"or "As the sheriff of this town, I demand you all come together."

Mull T. Ply (multiplication)–Like Addy, he helped to create more. "You make me feel like twice the man I am," or "With my help we can take this posse and double our strength."
Subb (subtraction)–Whenever he was around, people felt diminished. "I want the sum of you to split," or "Wherever you go, I'll take a part of you with me."
Div (division)–He divided a big, happy family into smaller groups. "Sometimes I feel as if I am the cause of families breaking up." "My plan is to divide and conquer."

4. Act It Out

Either with puppets or playing the characters themselves, the students share their scenarios.

The Dramatically Different Classroom • Christine Laitta & Mark Weakland
Kagan Publishing • 1 (800) WEE CO-OP • www.KaganOnline.com

Place Your Order

Students use math calculation, number sense, and problem-solving skills to complete a purchase order for materials appropriate for a math classroom.

1. Model It

Model the process of completing a purchase order. Stress how students have to consider not only what the classroom needs, but how much money they have.

2. Give an Example

Go through a magazine with the class and discuss what items you might purchase. Using a purchase order, show them where you would list the items and how you would calculate the total for the order.

3. Group Students

Group students in pairs or in groups of four.

4. Purchase Materials

Students work to complete their order forms and stay within the teacher's set parameters.

5. Share

Individuals and groups share their purchase orders with others and discuss how their orders are the same and different.

Stuff You Need

- Catalogs, old and/or new, that contain math materials appropriate for a math classroom (about 15 or 20)
- Teacher-made purchase order form or actual order forms from the school or catalogs
- Calculators

Stuff You Need to Know

Students will need to have a basic understanding of adding and multiplying, be able to use a calculator and have some problem-solving skills. Before the activity you may want to add some parameters, such as students have to order more than six items but less than twenty and they can't spend more than $300 dollars.

Enhancers

- Have students buy materials for more than one class.
- Increase the amount of money that they can spend and have them calculate sales tax and shipping.
- In order to "open" their own store, students bring in a copy of their favorite mail order catalogs and place mock orders to create stock for their store.

Multiple Intelligences

- Logical/Mathematical
- Verbal/Linguistic
- Interpersonal

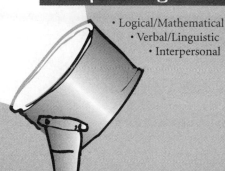

The Dramatically Different Classroom • Christine Laitta & Mark Weakland
Kagan Publishing • 1 (800) WEE CO-OP • www.KaganOnline.com

125

The Math Shack

Using straws, tape, and manila card stock or poster board, students construct a "shack" and share their discoveries about measurement with others. Building the shack promotes the use of measuring skills, math calculations, number sense, problem-solving strategies, and teamwork.

Stuff You Need

- Straws (10 to 20 per student)
- Poster board or new/old manila folders (one sheet per student)
- Tape
- Scissors (for each student)
- Teacher-made directions/dimensions for the shack
- Math Shack Blueprint blackline master

Stuff You Need to Know

In this activity the straws are two-by-fours, the poster board is the plywood, the tape is the nails, and the scissors are the saws. This activity takes a little preparation, but it's fun and great for exercising the students' spatial, calculating and problem-solving skills.

Enhancers

- Give additional problem-solving questions, such as what is the area of your roof in square inches or how many inches of gutter would you need to go around your roof.
- Give dimensions in feet, not in inches. Students will have to translate to scale.
- Give more particulars in your directions/dimensions, such as the roof has to be at a 30-degree angle or the total area of your windows cannot exceed 20 percent of the area of the shack.
- Build a shack from precut and reusable two-by-fours and plywood.

Multiple Intelligences

- Logical/Mathematical
- Verbal/Linguistic
- Visual/Spatial
- Interpersonal
- Bodily/Kinesthetic

1. Prepare Materials

The easiest way to prepare the materials is to have the students follow the directions on the Math Shack Blueprint blackline master. All of the needed materials and dimensions are given on this sheet. However, you may wish to create your own Math Shack. In this case, have students cut the straws and construction paper to your own dimensions or prepare and pre-cut enough straws and pieces of poster board to supply the anticipated number of student groups. Make sure you cut many of the straw pieces too small! The goal is to have the students "nail" small pieces together to come up with the correct dimensions. For example, if your walls are to be 10 inches tall, cut the straws in lengths of 5 inches, 3 inches, 7 inches and 2 inches.

2. Give Dimensions and Directions

Pass out the teacher-made directions and dimensions (or the Math Shack Blueprint blackline master) and review the directions with the class. You may want to have a second set of more challenging directions on hand for groups that finish early.

3. Form Groups

You may choose any of the following configurations: students alone, in pairs or in groups of three or four.

4. Build the Shack

Circulate around the room and provide side coaching and encouragement while the students build their shacks.

5. Share

At an appointed time, have the groups or individuals pair up with others and share their shacks. They explain how they built their shacks and compare and contrast with each other.

The Dramatically Different Classroom • Christine Laitta & Mark Weakland
Kagan Publishing • 1 (800) WEE CO-OP • www.KaganOnline.com

Math Shack Blueprint

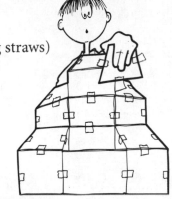

List of tools and materials:
- Plywood = construction paper (three 9 x 12-inch pieces)
- 2 x 4 boards = Straws (fifteen 9-inch long straws)
- Saw = Scissors (one per group or person)
- Nails = Scotch tape

Measurement Tips:
Measure twice, cut once!
Plan your 2 x 4 pieces before you cut them!
Plan your plywood pieces before you cut them out!

To build the Math Shack, cut the 2 x 4 boards (straws) into the following:

☐ Sixteen 2 x 4 boards, each one 6 inches long (for the wall frames)
☐ Three 2 x 4 boards, each one 8 inches long (for the roof posts and beam)

To build the Math Shack, cut the plywood (construction paper) into the following:

☐ Five pieces of plywood, each one 6 x 6 inches (for the walls and floor)
☐ Four pieces of plywood, each one 3 inches wide by 5 inches long (for the roof)
☐ Two pieces of plywood in the shape of a triangle, each one 6 inches long at the base and 2 inches high at the center (for the attic)

Here are the dimensions of the Math Shack:

- The Math Shack is 6 inches wide, 6 inches high and 6 inches deep.
- The front of the shack has a center-post that is 8 inches high.
- The back of the shack also has an 8 inch center post. Running from one post to the other is an 8-inch support beam. The shack has an attic formed from two triangles. It is topped by a slanted roof.

Construction Tip: Make your frames first, then attach the plywood!

Here are the construction instructions.

1. Construct frames for the four walls by making four 6 x 6-inch squares out of 2 x 4 boards.
2. Attach the four 6 x 6-inch squares together with nails to make a cube, 6 inches high, 6 inches wide and 6 inches deep.
3. Attach two 8-inch high center posts to the front and back walls.
4. Run an 8-inch beam from one center post to the other. This is the roof support.
5. Attach plywood to cover the floor and the four walls.
6. Attach the plywood triangles to form the attic walls.
7. Attach the roof.

Good luck!

The Dramatically Different Classroom • Christine Laitta & Mark Weakland
Kagan Publishing • 1 (800) WEE CO-OP • www.KaganOnline.com

127

How Many Borps in a Mile?

Students discover properties about measurement when they create and name their own unit of measurement. When they use their original unit to measure objects, they practice measuring and calculation, and use math reasoning to make effective decisions.

Stuff You Need

- String (enough for each child to have up to five feet)
- Teacher-made list of objects to be measured

Stuff You Need to Know

This activity is easily adapted up or down the ability spectrum and can include fractions and decimals (see Enhancers). Students should have a basic knowledge of measurement systems (standard or metric) and should be familiar with measuring objects. When constructing a list of the objects to be measured, the teacher should start with easy to find objects.

Enhancers

- Increase the size and number of objects to be measured. The students will need to create two or even three separate units of measurement and then pick the appropriate measure for the appropriate object.
- Measure objects to the nearest fraction of the unit and incorporate fractions.
- Measure objects to the nearest tenth of the unit and incorporate decimals.

Multiple Intelligences

- Logical/Mathematical
- Verbal/Linguistic
- Bodily/Kinesthetic
- Interpersonal
- Visual/Spatial

1. Model It

Explain that in this activity students will be creating their own unit of measurement. This unit will be based on an everyday object and will be used over and over again to measure length, height, and width. Model your examples. Here are three possibilities:

- One Borp = a piece of string the length of four math books laid end to end.
- One Biff = a piece of string as long as your knuckles when you make a fist.
- One Bitty = a piece of string the length of your small toe.

2. Teacher Measures

Using your created measurement, like a Biff, measure something like your shoe. "Look class, my shoe is about 3 Biffs long!"

3. Group Students

Group them as you see fit or have them work alone.

4. Give a Little List

Give students a list of objects to be measured.

5. Create a Unit

Students should consider the size of the objects on their list. They then pick an object that would serve as a good basis for their new unit of measurement. For example, a student would not want to measure the length of a hallway with a measurement unit the size of a toothbrush. Students then cut a piece of string as long as their base object and name the unit.

6. Measure It

Students measure objects found on their list.

7. Share and Share Alike

Students pair up with at least one other team and share and compare results. Then regroup for a class discussion. Pose these questions: Why do the results differ among the groups? Why is measurement standardized?

The Dramatically Different Classroom • Christine Laitta & Mark Weakland
Kagan Publishing • 1 (800) WEE CO-OP • www.KaganOnline.com

Build It With Bodies

Teacher and students stand and move to create a physical representation of a math formula, thereby adding visual elements to the lesson and making the abstract more concrete. Bodily, visual, spatial, and logical intelligences are all used in this activity.

1. Rewrite the Formula

Rewrite each letter or number of the math formula on large pieces of poster board or paper, one letter or number per piece. Make more than one copy of each formula element so that everyone in the class will have a piece of the formula. For example if you are working on the area of circles and your formula is $C = \pi r^2$, make multiple copies of C, π, r and a couple of = signs.

2. Introduce the Formula

Introduce the formula to the class and discuss its elements. Then pass out the elements of the formula to the class. As you hand each student the letter, number, or symbol, you may want to ask him or her what it stands for. Make sure everyone gets a letter, number, or symbol.

3. Build It With Bodies

Ask a student with an equal sign to come to the front. Then ask for a volunteer to come to the front and stand on either the right or the left side of the equal sign. Continue to build the formula until all of the students are in the correct position. Discuss the equation. Have these students sit and ask for other volunteers to make the formula on their own. Make sure they tell the class what they stand for before they place themselves in the formula.

4. Explore and Discover

Guide the class as they discover new relationships within the formula. For instance, if the teacher moves the C from one side of the equal sign to the other, will the other elements have to move? If so, where? If you place a D (diameter) on one side of the equal sign, what students belong on the other side?

5. Group Review

Once students know the process, allow them to problem solve in small groups. Monitor students as they review.

The Dramatically Different Classroom • Christine Laitta & Mark Weakland
Kagan Publishing • 1 (800) WEE CO-OP • www.KaganOnline.com

Stuff You Need

- Large note cards, pieces of poster board, construction paper, or scrap sheets of 8 1/2 inch by 11 inch pieces of paper (at least 20 to 30, or one for each student)
- Markers

Stuff You Need to Know

In this activity, students are guided by the teacher as they create a physical representation of a math formula.

Enhancers

- Assign students to help "direct" the formation of the formulas.
- Have students group themselves into correct formulas. How many of the formulas can you make at one time?
- Give each student a different number. Explore variations of number sentences. For example, if 7+2 stand on one side of the equals, what two other people must stand on the opposite side?
- Increase or decrease the grade levels of the formulas. Try algebraic equations, such as $4x + 2 = 3x + 7$.

Multiple Intelligences

- Logical/Mathematical
- Verbal/Linguistic
- Bodily/Kinesthetic
- Interpersonal

Tower of London

After looking at an existing model of a block tower, students form a construction group and work to re-create the model tower. Working together as an ensemble, students practice communication skills, logical reasoning, and use their spatial intelligence.

Stuff You Need

- Large variety of colored wooden blocks or Legos, Duplos, etc.
- Rulers (one per group)
- Paper and pencil (one per group)

Stuff You Need to Know

This is a role play activity for older students. The teacher must model the problems that will occur if teams have unrealistic expectations and a lack of communication. Solutions and methods of team communication should also be modeled for the class. The first tower should be simple enough so that all of the teams experience success! The teacher acts as the landowner who wants to have a new house or tower built. The students take on the roles of members in a construction group. They must follow these specific rules:

- **Contractor:** Talks only to the foreman, can look at the model house, measure it, and take notes about it.
- **Foreman:** Can talk to both the contractor and the workers, and can look at the contractor's notes. Cannot take the notes to the work site or show them to the workers.
- **Workers:** Can only talk to each other, cannot look at the notes. Because of the constraints of each member of the construction group, part of each student's task is to create a positive and appreciative work environment.

1. Form Teams

Each team needs to have five people: one contractor, one foreman, and three workers. After grouping students into fives, the teacher assigns them jobs. Students should be able to tell the teacher how they are going to make the job go smoothly for their co-workers. For example, the foreman tells the contractor that the workers need more time and the contractor agrees to go back to the tower and remeasure it when this is requested by the foreman.

2. Contractor Measures Tower

The team sends out the contractor to look at the model tower. It is up to the contractor to measure the tower, note color and placement of blocks, draw diagrams, etc.

3. Contractor and Foreman Discuss

The contractor goes back to the foreman and discusses the tower with him or her and shares notes and diagrams.

4. Foreman and Workers Discuss

The foreman talks to the workers and explains how the tower should be built. However, the foreman cannot show the workers the diagram or notes and the workers cannot talk back to the foreman. Workers can talk among themselves to clarify and/or discuss the foreman's directions. It is up to them to work out how they will place the blocks.

The Dramatically Different Classroom • Christine Laitta & Mark Weakland
Kagan Publishing • 1 (800) WEE CO-OP • www.KaganOnline.com

5. Teacher Side Coaches

Walk through the room and side coach: "Looks good. I like the way this team is working together." "I like the way these workers are helping each other move the blocks." Remember that the workers cannot talk to the foreman. "I think the contractor needs to go back and look at the tower," etc.

6. Take a Look

When the team is done building, allow them all to travel and take a look at the tower. Does the newly constructed one match the model?

7. Discuss

Discuss the project as a class or in small groups.

- What was difficult about the assignment?
- Was anything easy?
- What skills were most important?
- What would have helped make the project go more smoothly?
- What was learned about communication?
- What was difficult in each particular job?
- How is this project like and/or unlike the real workplace?

Enhancers

- Switch group members and discuss what you have learned by doing someone else's job.
- Build the tower using more blocks. Change the plane of some of the blocks.
- Increase the difficulty level by making a house from different shaped blocks placed in different configurations.

Multiple Intelligences

- Logical/Mathematical
- Verbal/Linguistic
- Bodily/Kinesthetic
- Interpersonal
- Visual/Spatial

The Dramatically Different Classroom • Christine Laitta & Mark Weakland
Kagan Publishing • 1 (800) WEE CO-OP • www.KaganOnline.com

131

Movement Review

Students take a break and get a little exercise as they use their bodies to review math facts and concepts. While engaged in this activity, students are working on building an ensemble as well as their mathematical skills.

Stuff You Need

- Math concepts and facts currently being studied or previously studied, such as the communicative property, addition facts, place values, and fractions
- Large number cards for students to hold
- Large symbol cards (with +, =, x, a decimal point, etc)
- A clear space

Stuff You Need to Know

The teacher may want to build in a small amount of time (five to ten minutes) each day to do this activity. It works best if done each day. Modify this activity based on the size of your class, the maturity level of the students and their knowledge of the concept or fact you are reviewing. One management strategy you could use in this activity is to remind students that numbers and symbols don't talk! All group work and movement must be done silently.

1. Organize the Class

Divide the class into sections that can be easily called upon. If the class is in rows, make sure that each row knows its number. If the class is configured in groups at tables, give each a number.

2. Ideas for Movement

Think of and/or write down math facts and concepts that could be demonstrated through movement of bodies. Starting with simple facts is easiest. Facts and concepts can be written on cards (for the teacher or a student to randomly pull) or everything can simply be kept right on the cerebral cortex. Here are some ideas:

- **The communicative property:** $5 + 4 = 4 + 5$ or $2 \times 3 = 3 \times 2$.
- **Place value:** ones, tens, hundreds, thousands, millions.
- **Addition facts:** $3 + 4 = 7$
- **Fractions:** Fractions of a set, fractions of a whole.

The Dramatically Different Classroom • Christine Laitta & Mark Weakland
Kagan Publishing • 1 (800) WEE CO-OP • www.KaganOnline.com

3. Call It Out

Call on a group of students to demonstrate a particular fact or concept. Here are some examples based on the previous ideas:

- The teacher says "Groups 2 and 3, show me the communicative property using 4 + 5." The tables group themselves into a group of 4 and a group of 5 students. A student with an addition sign stands in the middle. Then the groups switch places.
- The teacher says "Table 5, make the number 3,405." Table 5 picks the four needed numbers and a comma, stands up and forms the number. Teacher then says "Sit down if you're in the hundred's place, jump if you are in the one's place and make a funny face if you are in the ten's place" or "Now make the biggest number you can from your given numbers."
- Teacher says "Rows 1 and 3, show me the fact 13 − 7 = 6." Thirteen students in Rows 1 and 3 combine to make a group of 13. Seven then sit down. Six remain.

Enhancers

- Keep a card file on the concepts that the class has learned. Each time a new concept is learned, add it to the file. Pull out cards as needed to review.

Multiple Intelligences

- Bodily/Kinesthetic
- Interpersonal
- Logical/Mathematical
- Visual/Spatial

The Dramatically Different Classroom • Christine Laitta & Mark Weakland
Kagan Publishing • 1 (800) WEE CO-OP • www.KaganOnline.com

133

All in the Family

Wearing name tags containing math information instead of names, students discover math patterns among themselves. As they examine each person's name tag and discover members of their "math family," students practice number sense, problem solving, and logical thinking.

Stuff You Need

- "Hello, My Name Is..." name tags. These name tags can be the reusable kind (with a pin and transparent plastic sleeve) or the disposable sticky kind (one for each student)
- Fine-point markers of different colors

Stuff You Need to Know

This interactive activity allows students to work on ensemble as well as practice problem solving and number sense.

1. What Is the Math Family?

Before you begin to prepare the name tags, you will have to decide what type of pattern, family of facts, or category you want to create. **Here is an example of a family of facts:** 6 + 6, 3 + 9, 14 - 2, and 7 + 5 (all equal 12).

Here is an example of a pattern: 6, 3, 8, 5, 10, 7 (subtract 3 then add 5).

Here is an example of a category: 1/4, 0, 0.357, 1/8 (all are numbers less than one).

2. Choose an Option

Here are some options for preparing the name tags.

Option A: What's Your Family's Name?
Families are grouped together by colored name tags. Their job is to discover their family name. For example: Six students have red name tags that say "Hello, my name is 0.25" (or 1.357, 2.06, etc.). This family would discover they are the "Decimal Family." Six students have blue name tags that say "Hello, my name is 1/4" (or 2/8, 25/7, etc.). This family would discover they are the "Fraction Family."

The Dramatically Different Classroom • Christine Laitta & Mark Weakland
Kagan Publishing • 1 (800) WEE CO-OP • www.KaganOnline.com

Option B: Find Your Family

Families are mixed up and teacher asks them to find their family members. This works best if the family groups are readily apparent, say whole numbers and fractions or binomials and trinomials.

Option C: Family Problems

Families are grouped together, each knows what their name is, and the teacher directs them to work together to solve a problem. For example: "All families, put yourself in order from the smallest value member to the largest value," or "Fraction family, find your brother or sister in the decimal family" (1/4 would pair with 0.25, 1/2 would pair with 0.5).

3. Prepare Name Tags

Teacher prepares the name tags.

4. Family Reunion

Students are placed in groups and are given directions. The groups of students then work together to solve the math problem and find out who their family is or how their family works.

The Dramatically Different Classroom • Christine Laitta & Mark Weakland
Kagan Publishing • 1 (800) WEE CO-OP • www.KaganOnline.com

135

Building an Arch

In this activity, students build an arch using their bodies. Abstract concepts such as compression and tension are made concrete as students creatively solve problems, communicate, and work as an ensemble.

Stuff You Need

- Examples of different styles of arches and buttresses and how they are made
- Examples of the mathematics underlying arches and buttresses (for upper level math classes)
- Examples of how arches are used (bridges and doorways)
- Photos of arches used in buildings in their community (teacher or student supplied)
- A large clear space to move in

Stuff You Need to Know

As they create the arch, students must keep a constant line of communication open in order to keep it from falling.

1. Review Concepts of Design

Review the following terms with students: "Tension," "Compression," "Support," "Counterbalance," "Buttresses" and "Distribution."

2. Mismatch Partners

Each student finds a partner that is either much shorter or much taller then him- or herself. Next, students lean from the waist with their hands above their heads, touching their partner's hands. The space between the students should be as wide as possible. Forming a human arch should be difficult to accomplish, proving the point that when building an arch the weight must be equal on each side. If you have a teeter totter on your playground, use it to demonstrate the same idea.

3. What Happened?

Sit in a circle and discuss what happened when partners were mismatched. Challenge the class to discover what would happen to a real arch.

- What would happen to the structure in the long run?
- How would the elements (rain, snow, and wind) affect the arch?
- How does the choice of building materials affect the arch?
- What do you need to create so the arch doesn't buckle?
- How does a keystone function in an arch?

4. Perfect Partners

Now have students find a partner close to their size and repeat the activity.

The Dramatically Different Classroom • Christine Laitta & Mark Weakland
Kagan Publishing • 1 (800) WEE CO-OP • www.KaganOnline.com

5. Compare

Sit in a circle again and discuss what was different. Why was it easier this time?

6. Add Buttresses

Now use some of the students as the buttresses. Place one student on each side of the arch with their backs against the backs of the students being the arch.

7. Discuss Improvement

Sit your students in a circle and discuss the added benefits of adding buttresses.

- What did they do for the arch itself?
- What are the long-term benefits?
- What building materials could they be made of?

8. Build an Arch

Using whatever type of materials you deem appropriate, have students build an arch. Possible materials are blocks, corrugated cardboard, glue, Styrofoam, bricks and anything else their imaginations can come up with.

9. Test for Strength

Have students agree on several levels of stress tests that they will put their arches through.

Enhancers

- Draw a connection between students' physical arches and the arches that exist within a community. Challenge students to think of other "arches" people create, such as volunteer programs, hospital helpers, Scout programs, Big Brothers/Big Sisters, and the Peace Corps.
- Build a bridge and test its strength.

Multiple Intelligences

- Verbal/Linguistic
- Visual/Spatial
- Bodily/Kinesthetic
- Interpersonal
- Logical/Mathematical
- Intrapersonal

The Dramatically Different Classroom • Christine Laitta & Mark Weakland
Kagan Publishing • 1 (800) WEE CO-OP • www.KaganOnline.com

137

Architecture That Works

After experiencing what it's like to have a physical disability and researching building codes and the law, students learn to recognize areas of their school that can be made more accessible to people with disabilities. Teams of students then design modifications to the school. This cross-curricular activity incorporates mathematics, law, government, architecture, and community.

Stuff You Need

- Wheelchairs
- Crutches
- Leg braces
- Neck braces
- Construction Action Plan blackline master

Stuff You Need to Know

This activity goes beyond simple role playing. It requires a commitment on the part of the students and other teachers in the school. Ideally, students should take turns throughout the day experiencing a specific handicap. Their obstacles will include opening doors, dealing with stairs, maneuvering in crowds, drinking from a fountain, and much more. The stuff you need (see above) may be borrowed from a local hospital, home for the elderly, school nurse or a medical supply store. The longer you have the teaching aids, the greater the impact.

1. Brainstorm Challenges

Have students generate a list of challenges that people with disabilities face when trying to get around in the school and community.

2. Pick a Challenge

Students randomly pick a challenge from a hat or box. For example, "while sitting in a wheelchair, get to your next class on time with all your needed supplies. Then report to the nurse's station to pick up your next challenge at noon."

3. Experience It

Students go out into the classroom and the school and experience what it is like to have a physical disabilitiy.

4. Discuss the Challenge

Sit in a circle and have students share their experiences. List the problems and frustrations students faced.

5. Discover the Existing Laws

Guide students as they gather information on laws that are designed to protect and ensure the rights of people with disabilities. Allow them to use the Internet, the school library, and any other community resources to research these laws.

The Dramatically Different Classroom • Christine Laitta & Mark Weakland
Kagan Publishing • 1 (800) WEE CO-OP • www.KaganOnline.com

6. List the Laws

Have students generate a list of existing laws that deal with architectural design and accommodating people with disabilities.

- What are the requirements for buildings?
- Are the laws well developed and fair?
- Do building laws change from state to state?

7. Make a Difference

Discover an area in your school that could be adapted for people with disabilities. Remember to inform your principal and let her or him know of the plans. For example:

- Build a ramp to get to a part of the school that has been unreachable in the past.
- Build easy access lockers.

The students' goal is to improve the quality of life for future students who may have handicaps.

8. Design It

With the teacher's guidance, students draft a construction plan that shows how a model of their improvement will be put together. Remember that the improvements should maintain or complement the style of the existing structure.

9. Students List Materials

With the teacher's guidance, the students (as a group) generate a list of materials. Hardware stores and other local businesses may want to donate some materials.

10. Teacher Assigns Tasks

Form the students into groups of four. Designate a specific area for each group to meet and work in.

11. Build the Model

Build the model to scale, testing it as you go. Have the students refer to the construction documents they have done so that they can piece the project together. Students then share their process and final product with others.

12. Celebrate

When the project is complete, have a party to unveil it and place a "plaque" with your architects' names on it.

Enhancers

- Chart or graph the progress of the groups.
- Have students journal their experiences.
- Challenge your students to approach the school board for improvement funds.
- Write your congressperson for support.

Multiple Intelligences

- Verbal/Linguistic
- Logical/Mathematical
- Visual/Spatial
- Intrapersonal
- Bodily/Kinesthetic
- Interpersonal

The Dramatically Different Classroom • Christine Laitta & Mark Weakland
Kagan Publishing • 1 (800) WEE CO-OP • www.KaganOnline.com

139

Construction Action Plan

Group members_____

☐ Engage in an experience that gives you a greater understanding of the challenges facing a person with a disability.

☐ Make a list of challenges you encountered during your experience. Pay special attention to any areas in the school that were difficult to navigate.

☐ Share your experiences with another student or group of students.

☐ Research and learn about the laws that pertain to making buildings accessible.

☐ Discover an area in your school that could be adapted for someone with a disability.

☐ Propose a way to make this area more accessible for someone with a disability.

☐ With a group of students, draft a construction plan that shows how a model of your improvement will be put together.

☐ Build a scale model of your project.

☐ Share your proposal, construction plans, and model with another student or group of students.

The Dramatically Different Classroom • Christine Laitta & Mark Weakland
Kagan Publishing • 1 (800) WEE CO-OP • www.KaganOnline.com

Teacher for a Day

When they become a teacher for a day, students experience all the planning and self-expression that goes into developing a math lesson. This activity, which can be applied to any school subject, promotes creativity, self-confidence, and leadership, and promotes in-depth understanding of the material students will be teaching.

1. Select the Teacher(s)

Students will have to demonstrate their preparedness to the teacher before they can begin to teach, so make sure they know what is expected. Lots of advance notice and concrete guidelines help to give struggling learners a chance to teach, too. The teacher can choose one student or a team of two or three students. Encourage students to teach something that they really enjoy and are good at.

2. Create a Time Line

Give students a time frame in which each element of the lesson should be completed. Several due dates will teach them to manage their time.

3. Students Plan Their Lesson

Using the Lesson Plan blackline, students plan their lessons.

4. Dry Run

Encourage students to practice their lesson with a partner or another group. Remind them to time their presentation so it does not go over allotted class time.

5. Students Teach the Class

Have the students teach the lesson.

Stuff You Need

- A lesson plan outlining what the student needs to cover in their lesson
- Lesson Plan blackline master

Stuff You Need to Know

Introducing students to teaching allows them access to a valuable tool they will use over and over again. As every teacher knows, a person must be thoroughly familiar with material before he or she can effectively teach it. The teacher supplies the "meat" of the lesson and gives the student a lesson outline that helps each one to organize his or her thoughts and plans. The student must provide any aids that are needed for the completed lesson. The teacher may also wish to give a set of parameters to the student instead of leaving the lesson design and content totally open. For example:
- Teach multiplication of 6s
- Use rhythm as a technique
- Review and quiz students without a written test

Enhancers

- Have the students plan an entire lesson on their own.

Multiple Intelligences

- Verbal/Linguistic
- Visual/Spatial
- Bodily/Kinesthetic
- Interpersonal
- Intrapersonal
- Musical/Rhythmic
- Logical/Mathematical

The Dramatically Different Classroom • Christine Laitta & Mark Weakland
Kagan Publishing • 1 (800) WEE CO-OP • www.KaganOnline.com

141

Lesson Plan

Name_____

1. What is the title of your lesson?

_____

2. List one or two objectives for your lesson. These are the things you expect your students to be able to do after you are done teaching them.

_____

_____

_____

3. How will you begin your lesson?

_____

_____

_____

4. What will be the main activity during your lesson?

_____

_____

_____

_____

5. As you teach your students, how will you check to see if they are learning?

_____

_____

_____

_____

The Dramatically Different Classroom • Christine Laitta & Mark Weakland
Kagan Publishing • 1 (800) WEE CO-OP • www.KaganOnline.com

6. How will your students practice what they have learned?

_____

_____

_____

7. How will you end your lesson?

_____

_____

_____

8. Will you assign homework? If you do, what will it be?

_____

_____

9. List any special ways of teaching or any special things you will do to help students who may not understand your lesson.

_____

_____

_____

_____

10. List all of the materials that you will need for your lesson. Will you need a textbook, hands-on materials, an overhead, special materials, or anything else?

_____

_____

_____

_____

_____

_____

X_____

Cooperating Teacher's Signature and Date

AUTO-HOMEWORK DOER (STATION)

Architects:
Making a Difference

When they take on the role of an architectural firm (ensemble), students brainstorm, design, and build an item that has a practical use for the classroom. This cross-curricular activity integrates mathematics, science, and architecture. It inspires creative problem solving, teamwork, cooperation, planning, and self-confidence.

Stuff You Need

- Building materials, such as foam board, corrugated cardboard, Styrofoam or other lightweight materials
- Wood, nails, wood glue, measuring tape, sander, hammers
- A person trained in carpentry
- Glue, tape, scissors
- Art supplies to decorate the final project

Stuff You Need to Know

Architecture is a collection of parts and pieces working together (like an ensemble). This activity needs to be tailored to the age of your students. It can be as simple or as complex as you need it to be. The important point is that the class is creating a project as an ensemble.

1. Brainstorm

The first step is to have students generate ideas of something their classroom could use. The size and difficulty of the project will depend on the grade level. Here are some ideas to get you going.
- Reading nook
- Coat rack
- Listening station
- Filing system
- Fantasy space
- Corinthian columns (every classroom needs these)

2. Students Design

Students put together a schematic design. This is their concept for the space or item that they are designing. This can be a collage, painting, scale drawing or photos that are shown during a verbal presentation.

3. Act It Out

Have each student present his or her idea and then act out what takes place in the new space or how they will use the new object. The students "act out" the scenario in order to make their abstract idea concrete.

4. Choose a Subject

Have students vote on the space or object that would benefit the class the most. Make it clear this is not a competition. It is a time to decide as an ensemble what would be helpful, inspiring, and reasonable to create.

5. List Your Materials

With the teacher's guidance, students (as a group) generate a list of all their needs. For example: to make a poetry corner they will need fabric, pillows, poetry books, a book rack, paints, and mood lighting.

The Dramatically Different Classroom • Christine Laitta & Mark Weakland
Kagan Publishing • 1 (800) WEE CO-OP • www.KaganOnline.com

6. Form Groups

Put students into groups of four. Designate an area for each group to meet and work in.

7. Draft Construction Documents

With your aid and guidance, students draft a construction document that shows how their tasks will be completed and then assembled.

8. Assign Specific Tasks

Students are given specific tasks to complete based on the construction documents. For example, if the class is building a poetry corner, one group sews the pillows together, one group collects poetry and puts it into a book format, one group makes lamp shades, etc.

9. Test Your Structure

If you are building a platform or something that the students will be leaning against, sitting on or standing on top of, you must test each component as you build it.

10. Put It Together

Have students bring it all together by combining the final products.

11. Celebrate Your New Addition

When they have finished, have a party to unveil the space or object. Then place a "plaque" with the names of the architects on it.

Enhancers

- Take this activity down a grade level by eliminating steps such as drafting.
- Chart progress on a separate board.
- Have the class journal their experience.
- Challenge your students to design, draft, and build their own projects. Pick a theme that is specific to their personal talents.

Multiple Intelligences

- Verbal/Linguistic
- Visual/Spatial
- Bodily/Kinesthetic
- Interpersonal
- Logical/Mathematical
- Intrapersonal

The Dramatically Different Classroom • Christine Laitta & Mark Weakland
Kagan Publishing • 1 (800) WEE CO-OP • www.KaganOnline.com

145

Science and Health

(Safety Goggles and Rubber Gloves)

The Dramatically Different Classroom • Christine Laitta & Mark Weakland
Kagan Publishing • 1 (800) WEE CO-OP • www.KaganOnline.com

147

Soaring Through the Solar System

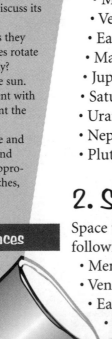

Through role playing and the use of manipulatives, students learn the relative sizes and distances of the planets. This activity teaches science facts and involves the bodily/kinesthetic and spatial intelligences.

Stuff You Need

- A basketball or large yellow volleyball and two golf balls
- A chart or poster of the planets' size, shape, distance, and general qualities
- Pictures of the planets
- Tape measure
- Poster board, markers, tape (to create distance markers) or traffic cones
- Clay, balloons, rulers, and paper-clips

Stuff You Need to Know

Manipulatives and movements are excellent ways to turn abstract concepts into concrete examples. You should thoroughly discuss the term "scale model" before you do this lesson.

Enhancers

- Get fancy and demonstrate how space probes use planetary mass to increase their velocity.
- Stop at each planet and discuss its characteristics.
- Have the planets rotate as they stand in place. Which ones rotate quickly, which ones slowly?
- Have the planets orbit the sun.
- Decorate the actual student with craft materials to represent the surface of the planet.
- Give students the real size and distances of the planets and have them calculate an appropriate scale model (in inches, feet and/or yards).

Multiple Intelligences

- Verbal/Linguistic
- Visual/Spatial
- Bodily/Kinesthetic
- Interpersonal
- Logical/Mathematical
- Naturalist

1. Create the Planets

Make representations of the planets using clay and balloons. Put the planets on sticks, rulers, or paper clips for easy handling. Here are the sun and planet scaled-down sizes:

- The Sun = a basketball!
- Mercury = 0.5 centimeters
- Venus = 2.5 cm
- Earth = 2.5 cm
- Mars = 1.0 cm
- Jupiter = 13 cm balloon
- Saturn = 12 cm balloon
- Uranus = a golf ball
- Neptune = a golf ball
- Pluto = 0.5 cm

2. Space the Planets

Space the planets apart using the following dimensions:

- Mercury = 6 m from the sun
- Venus = 10 m
- Earth = 15 m
- Mars = 23 m
- Jupiter = 77 m
- Saturn = 140 m
- Uranus = 285 m
- Neptune = 450 m
- Pluto = 595 m

Use traffic cones or other easily visible markers to identify the placement of each planet. You will need a large open space such as a football field, parking lot, or playground. For the most distant planets you may want to place them at the outer boundary of your open space and indicate their distance rather than use the actual distance since Pluto would be nearly six football fields away.

3. Cast Your Characters/Planets

You will need one student for the sun and nine others for planets. Place the students at the appropriate cones. The rest of the students are the space probes. Either starting from the sun or from the Earth, conduct a planetary flyby. This involves running across the field and past the planets.

The Dramatically Different Classroom • Christine Laitta & Mark Weakland
Kagan Publishing • 1 (800) WEE CO-OP • www.KaganOnline.com

Bunsen Burners & Other Hot Topics

Students create a science talk show in which some of the students are guests and others are the questioning "studio" audience. A talk show is a great way to test science or health comprehension without a written exam. It also challenges students to think on their feet, put information into their own words, and develop self-expression.

1. Create the Questions

After telling students what guest (topic) will be appearing on the talk show, have them generate questions to ask the guest. For example, "Professor Einstein what is your greatest accomplishment?" "Tell us Professor what does $e=mc^2$ mean?"

2. Rehearse the Possibilities

Review the questions the class has prepared. Have students pair up and practice answering them.

3. Select Your Panel

Pick some students to be guests. If you are studying one topic, pick multiple guests to be the same topic and let them agree on the answer. For example, if you are studying the moon, five students appear as the moon. Some subject matter lends itself to many different guests. For example, if you are studying the periodic table you could have many students appear as different elements.

4. Create Audience Questions

The rest of the class will be the studio audience. Have the studio audience prepare questions to ask the guests. Now the teacher is the star of his or her very own show. Start with a little dialogue, such as "Welcome to *Back Talk*, brought to you by room 201. Today's guests are members of Periodic Table of the Elements..." applaud your guests.

5. Challenge the Audience

Switch the panel and the guests.

Stuff You Need

- Chairs placed in front of the room (one per guest)
- Prepared questions dealing with material your class has studied
- Index cards (with one question per card)

Stuff You Need to Know

Whatever or whoever the class is studying becomes the guest. If the topic is annelids or segmented worms, then the students become marine worms, earthworms, and leeches. The teacher, as the host of the show, provides the structure and management to the talk show. The questions and answers will reflect the students preparation and insight.

Enhancers

- Pick five people for each guest and rotate them in and out of the guest seat.
- Film as a video. During the filming of the show, put in room for a commercial break. ("This show is being brought to you by photosynthesis, dedicated to bringing the green to all plants.")
- During the replay of the talk show video, students could take a "break" to take a spelling test take or a bathroom break.

Multiple Intelligences

- Visual/Spatial
- Bodily/Kinesthetic
- Interpersonal
- Verbal/Linguistic
- Logical/Mathematical
- Naturalist

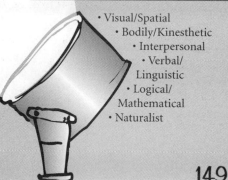

The Dramatically Different Classroom • Christine Laitta & Mark Weakland
Kagan Publishing • 1 (800) WEE CO-OP • www.KaganOnline.com

149

Let's Make It Move

Using movements and sounds, students create a human machine that demonstrates a scientific concept, such as friction, laws of motion, or gravity. This activity promotes creative problem solving and working as an ensemble, and allows students to use their logical/mathematical, visual/spatial, and bodily/kinesthetic intelligences.

Stuff You Need

• A clear space

Stuff You Need to Know

By choosing and adding students one at a time, the teacher manages the class and keeps the lesson flowing smoothly. Add each student after you ask, "What does your sound and movement represent?" and "How does it add to the final product?" Remember you are using the students' action and sound to represent the concept.

1. Discussion of Machines

Discuss how scientists use machines, robots, and computers in their laboratories and how machines help scientists produce products they would use in experimentation. Then remind students that each part of the machine must interrelate and is dependent upon every other part.

2. Discussion and Brainstorm

After discussing and or reviewing the science law, theory, or concept, brainstorm machines that demonstrate what is being studied.

3. Create the Movements and Sounds

After you settle on an idea for a machine, the teacher demonstrates how movement and sound go together. For example, if your machine is demonstrating friction, students may choose to rub their hands together and produce a rasping sound.

The Dramatically Different Classroom • Christine Laitta & Mark Weakland
Kagan Publishing • 1 (800) WEE CO-OP • www.KaganOnline.com

4. Students Create

Ask students to create movements and sounds that are specific to what is being made. Give them time to experiment.

5. Begin Building Your Machine

Now start building. Begin with someone doing a movement and a sound. Ask them what their specific job is in the machine. How will it affect the final creation? Place this student in the front and ask others "How can we add to it?"

6. Add Students One at a Time

Add students until the entire group is engaged. Encourage the ensemble to work together and interrelate.

7. Regulate Production

Slow down the machine by decreasing the speed/energy of the work. Continue to decrease it until the machine comes to rest.

Enhancers

• Speed it up, slow it down.
• Create simple machines for younger students and more complex machines for older students.

Multiple Intelligences

• Visual/Spatial
• Bodily/Kinesthetic
• Interpersonal
• Logical/Mathematical
• Musical/Rhythmic

The Dramatically Different Classroom • Christine Laitta & Mark Weakland
Kagan Publishing • 1 (800) WEE CO-OP • www.KaganOnline.com

151

Journey to the Center of the Earth

Storytelling and physically altering the classroom's appearance into the layers of the Earth allow the teacher and class to take an imaginary journey. While using imagination, storytelling techniques, improvisation skills, and creative problem-solving techniques, students also learn a lot about science and geology!

Stuff You Need

• Butcher paper (white paper on a large roll)
• Pictures of the Earth's crust and inner layers
• Rock samples, such as obsidian, sedimentary, basalt, granite, etc.
• Tape, markers, glue, dirt, and labels
• A list of obstacles that may arise (as you travel to the Earth's core)

Stuff You Need to Know

By transforming the classroom into the Earth's core, students literally learn from the inside out. The teacher must construct a story line on why the class is taking the journey, such as to collect rock samples for a museum. Discuss the possible dangers you may encounter when digging so far into the Earth. This activity leans heavily on the following techniques: side coaching, imagery, improvisation, and storytelling. The only difference between this activity and reading a story aloud is that the teacher creates the story and is up walking around the classroom.

1. Review Your Book Lesson

Review your lesson on geology/earth science and discuss important facts you will need to know, such as the size of the Earth, the layers and thickness of the Earth, and its temperatures.

2. Draw the Mural

Students create a mural that wraps around the classroom and depicts the Earth's surface, layers and core. The mural should include not only pictures of the layers but also facts about the rocks.

3. Choose Your Tools

Discuss what tools and supplies you will need for the journey. Discuss how you will retrieve the rocks and get them to the surface.

4. Tell the Story

Begin the trip. Be open to letting the story unfold as you go deeper and deeper into the Earth. You create the mood and obstacles for the travelers by explaining the changing rock layers and thickness, the depth at which you are traveling, and the temperature.

5. Head Home and Review

Return to the surface by reviewing the material as you "head home."

The Dramatically Different Classroom • Christine Laitta & Mark Weakland
Kagan Publishing • 1 (800) WEE CO-OP • www.KaganOnline.com

Or try this version!

1. Rearrange the Room

Push all the desks and students into a large circle, leaving the center of the room open.

2. Create the Core

Have four students sit in chairs in the center of the room. They should be grouped very tightly because the center of the Earth is very dense. Caution: make sure you don't say "these students are very dense!"

3. Create the Layers

Begin to construct a layer of desks around the dense core. As you finish a layer, discuss what the layer is called and composed of. You may want to hand out pictures of rock or actual rocks that may come from this layer to various students.

4. Dig Deeper

Add another layer to the Earth, forming concentric circles, and discuss. The walls of the room can be the surface of the Earth.

Simulate a Volcano

Have some students that make up the mantle get out of their seats and extrude or push through the line of seats in front of them (which is the crust). This represents a hot spot, such as a volcano, in the Earth's crust!

Simulate Tectonic Movement

Students sitting in the first line of desks, that make up the Earth's crust, get out of their seats and become subsumed or pushed under and back into the mantle. This is simply switching from the first line back to the second line of desks. In geology, this occurs because of movement of the Earth's plates (tectonic movements).

Enhancers

• Send a small team of two to three brave adventurers out of the room. Have them "drill" to the center of the Earth by first entering the Earth's crust through a hole in the Earth (the classroom door). As they drill through the Earth, they should report out loud what types of rocks they are encountering, how they feel, is the job easy or difficult, is it hot, etc.
• Write a play based on the story you create.
• Adapt this lesson for the biosphere.
• Adapt this lesson for the atmosphere.

Multiple Intelligences

• Verbal/Linguistic
• Visual/Spatial
• Bodily/Kinesthetic
• Interpersonal
• Naturalist

The Dramatically Different Classroom • Christine Laitta & Mark Weakland
Kagan Publishing • 1 (800) WEE CO-OP • www.KaganOnline.com

153

I Am a Tree

Students use their bodies in a connected formation to create a model of a living, working tree. Creating a tree made of students (a memorable way to teach a biology lesson) makes biology terms more understandable and helps students retain scientific facts and terms.

Stuff You Need

• Space to move around in, preferably outside

Stuff You Need to Know

The teacher facilitates the arrangement of students as they form the working model of a tree. If possible, do this activity outside in the presence of trees. If trees are nearby, you can start the lesson by explaining to students that the trees are working, like a factory, even though you cannot hear them. Remind students that this lesson pertains to deciduous trees, not coniferous.

Enhancers

• Demonstrate what happens to a tree in summer by having the students make their voices louder and make their movements more energetic. To demonstrate winter, have the students slow down and soften their speech and do their motions slowly.

Multiple Intelligences

• Verbal/Linguistic
• Visual/Spatial
• Bodily/
  Kinesthetic
• Interpersonal
• Naturalist

Note: This activity is based on an idea from the *McKeever Environmental Center's Earthkeepers Program.*

1. Get to a Tree

If you are near trees, go to them! Hug a tree, feel a tree, sit under a tree. If you are in an area with no trees, bring one to school. Almost everyone has a ficus tree (real or fake).

2. Review How a Tree Works

Take a few minutes to review any material you have previously studied on trees.

3. Make a Tree

The teacher will cast the following characters:

• **Roots:** Four or five students sit on the floor with their legs out. They repeat these words: "sip, sip..."
• **Heartwood:** The next group stands behind the roots. They place their right hand over their hearts and repeatedly say, "I am strong, I support."

• **Sapwood**: Made up of two tissue layers:
  • *Xylem (water tubes):* This group forms a circle around the heart wood and joins hands. While pumping their hands up and down, they say, "gurgle, gurgle, glug, glug."
  • *Phloem (food tubes):* This group forms a circle around the xylem with joined hands. While pumping their hands up and down, they say, "slurp, slurp, yum, yum."
• **Leaves:** This groups stands at the top of the tree with their arms and fingers outstretched. They say, "we make food, we make food."

4. Cut Down the Tree

The students playing the leaves fall slowly to the floor (and back to their respective seats). It's fall! The heart wood and sap wood are cut down by the teacher for firewood and return to their seats. The roots shrivel up in slow motion and disintegrate into the earth (or go to their seats).

154

The Dramatically Different Classroom • Christine Laitta & Mark Weakland
Kagan Publishing • 1 (800) WEE CO-OP • www.KaganOnline.com

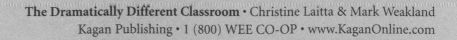

Family Tree

As students create a graph on poster board in the shape of a tree, they map out their family tree and discover how genetic traits are passed on. Students compare family traits on the tree, use their visual/spatial intelligence, and learn about the science of genetics.

1. Create the Tree

Develop a family tree that is large enough for each child's family. Explain which person would sit at the bottom and discuss how he tree grows with each new family member. Leave room for descriptions and/or photos of family members.

2. Fill in the Tree

Students fill in the tree and return it to school to create a forest of families in your classroom. Students can also use the Family Tree blackline to make observations about their families.

3. Hey, My Grandma Has My Eyes!

Have students discover similar traits that have been passed on from one generation to another.

4. Discuss and Share

Have students share what they have learned about how traits are passed on. Discover from where each child gets their eye color, hair color, etc.

Stuff You Need

- Access to facts about the physical traits of family members
- A piece of poster board (one per student)
- Markers
- Family Tree blackline master

Stuff You Need to Know

Students interview family members and fill in their physical traits as well as special talents. If a personal interview is difficult, encourage students to phone, talk with parents, and find old photos. Consider students who are adopted. How will this affect their tree?

Enhancers

- For younger students, keep the trees small and limited to the immediate family. For older students, allow them to go back in time as far as possible.
- Bring in your grandmother!

Multiple Intelligences

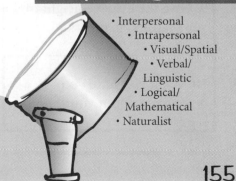

- Interpersonal
- Intrapersonal
- Visual/Spatial
- Verbal/Linguistic
- Logical/Mathematical
- Naturalist

The Dramatically Different Classroom • Christine Laitta & Mark Weakland
Kagan Publishing • 1 (800) WEE CO-OP • www.KaganOnline.com

155

Family Tree

	Mother's Side	Father's Side
1. What eye colors are in your family and who has them?		
2. What hair colors are in your family and who has them?		
3. Can people in your family curl their tongue? If so, who can do it?		
4. Who can sing?		
5. Are your earlobes attached or unattached?		
6. Who in your family is right-handed? Who is left-handed?		
7. Who in your family has toes that curl under? Who has toes that stick straight out?		
8. How many boys in your family? How many girls?		
9. Give the average height of your family members.		
10. What else have you discovered about your family?		

The Dramatically Different Classroom • Christine Laitta & Mark Weakland
Kagan Publishing • 1 (800) WEE CO-OP • www.KaganOnline.com

It's Alive

Students pick an object or organism currently being studied, such as an amoeba, and make it "real" by giving it human characteristics, such as a voice, a style of walking, and an attitude. This activity enables students to review facts in a fun and creative way.

1. Pick Your Theme

Have students choose a "character" and then create the story it will tell.

2. Discuss Writing Styles

Discuss students' options for the writing portion of the project. They can write the story of their character as a dialogue or monologue. Here is an example of a monologue:

"Hi, my name is Mars and boy do I feel red in the face. It's not because I'm embarrassed though. It's because my soil is full of rust. Scientists call it 'iron oxide.'

If you choose to do this as a small group activity, then dialogue will probably work best. What would a plant say to another plant about photosynthesis?

3. Prepare

Rehearse the dialogue/monologue.

4. Share

Have groups share with the class or with each other.

5. Critique

Discuss what worked best in each story.

Stuff You Need

- Science books with examples of amoebas, germs, atoms, planets, plants, animals, etc.
- Videos, slides, or pictures that would enhance the lesson

Stuff You Need to Know

This activity gives students a chance to use self-expression, humor, and insight by turning the abstract into a concrete idea. If you were an amoeba, what would you say? "I'll absorb you. Hey man, time to split!"

Enhancers

- Videotape the stories and create an "It's Alive Library."
- Write a play for the whole class based on the concept of things that are too small to see.
- Invite other science classes to your program. Later, discuss what they learned from it.

Multiple Intelligences

- Verbal/Linguistic
- Visual/Spatial
- Bodily/Kinesthetic
- Interpersonal
- Logical/Mathematical
- Naturalist

The Dramatically Different Classroom • Christine Laitta & Mark Weakland
Kagan Publishing • 1 (800) WEE CO-OP • www.KaganOnline.com

157

Stuff You Need

- CDs, cassettes, albums
- CD player, cassette player, etc.

Stuff You Need to Know

Music is the perfect way to break up a long block of time and still provide a "teaching moment." Discographies or collections of recordings and songs by an artist are dependent upon the age of the students, the course content, and the availability of resources and ideas. As you begin to collect songs, remember that they do not have to teach content but can merely enhance or reflect the content. Here are examples of songs and music that are not meant to teach content:

When studying geology *Landslide*-Fleetwood Mac; *Volcano*-Jimmy Buffet; *Ain't No Mountain High Enough*-Diana Ross

When studying weather systems *Clouds*-Joni Mitchell; *Stormy Weather*-Billie Holiday; *I Can See Clearly Now*-Johnny Nash

When studying chemistry *The Elements*-Tom Lehrer; *Song parodies* from Bill Nye the Science Guy

When doing independent seat work Mozart; Handel; Bach-especially the largo movements; Mood music, ambient music, nature sounds

When studying astronomy *The Sun*-They Might Be Giants; *The Planets*-Gustav Holtz; *Interplanet Janet*-School House Rock

Enhancers

- Have your students search for songs that would fit in with a theme. Playing a song selected by a student can be highly rewarding to that student.
- Create a collective discography in conjunction with your school library. Make it available to other teachers.

Multiple Intelligences

- Musical/Rhythmic
- Verbal/Linguistic
- Intrapersonal

Songs of Science

By playing theme-related music for the class, the teacher enhances the content of a current lesson. Although this activity does not teach content, simply supplementing the lesson, it appeals to students' musical intelligence, creates a lighter classroom atmosphere, and provides for a break in the busy day.

1. Create the Collection

Go through your music library and find songs that complement the lessons you are teaching.

2. Plan Your Lesson

As you plan your lessons, flip through your list of songs and see what you have filed under each subject. Try using a recipe box as a source guide. Remember to cross reference songs. For example, *Clouds* by Joni Mitchell, could be used to supplement a lesson on weather and could also be used to enhance a story about a complex interpersonal relationship (one in which there are "two sides" to each person's story).

3. Play the Music

Think of times to play the music in class. For example:

- As the students enter the room. This is a great management technique. When the music stops, it should be quiet and students should be ready to work.
- In the middle of a long block of time. Great for a break and a stretch.
- While students are working. Some research suggests that playing Mozart and Bach can actually improve a students ability to memorize and take tests.
- As students prepare to leave for the next class. This is a great time to play almost anything. You can turn your students on to a new jazz tune or the latest R and B hit.

The Dramatically Different Classroom • Christine Laitta & Mark Weakland
Kagan Publishing • 1 (800) WEE CO-OP • www.KaganOnline.com

Go With the Flow H₂O

Students sing and create movements that tell the story of the water cycle. Song and movements help students remember the components and sequence of the water cycle, and appeal to students' bodily/kinesthetic and musical intelligence.

Stuff You Need

- A list of familiar tunes that have easy-to-remember melodies
- Alternate lyrics printed on a handout (one per student)

Stuff You Need to Know

Creating science songs is easier than it might appear. Pick a familiar tune. List facts and concepts you want to cover in the song. Then arrange the content to fit the tune and you will have a fun and memorable song.

1. Review Lesson

After reading about the water cycle, take time to discuss the major points. For example, "When the water falls from the sky, what part of the water cycle is this?"

2. Sing Your Lesson

Have the students sing the water cycle song. For example, sing in the following words to the tune of *Oh, My Darling Clementine.* "Evaporation, condensation, precipitation all the time. This is called the water cycle and it happens all the time."

3. Choreograph It

Create gestures and or dance steps for the song. Have students suggest different movements.

Enhancers

- Apply these steps to create songs and choreography for other topics and multistep processes, such as a water purification or plant photosynthesis.
- Share your song with other science classes and see how much they retain.
- Record a CD of your class' greatest science hits.
- Have students generate their own science songs, lyrics, gestures, and dance.

Multiple Intelligences

- Verbal/Linguistic
- Visual/Spatial
- Bodily/ Kinesthetic
- Interpersonal
- Musical/ Rhythmic
- Naturalist

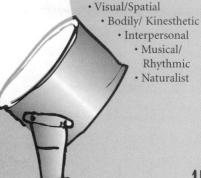

The Dramatically Different Classroom • Christine Laitta & Mark Weakland
Kagan Publishing • 1 (800) WEE CO-OP • www.KaganOnline.com

159

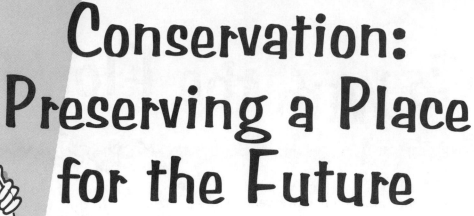

Conservation: Preserving a Place for the Future

Students find and conduct research on the local ecosystem to conserve local resources. This activity involves starting a petition, contacting a school board, writing to a member of Congress, giving speeches, campaigning and designing a proposal for designating the specific area a nature preserve. It also promotes communication, activism, leadership, working as an ensemble, and understanding local and state laws and regulations.

Stuff You Need

- A list of wild life that has been spotted in your area
- A chart listing the number of sightings of each animal or plant life
- Time for observation and discussion. Are there animals and plants that are in danger due to construction sites, housing developments or "the man?"
- A list of reasons why the area should be set aside for preservation
- A petition form
- Local Ecosystem Review blackline master
- Conservation Action Plan blackline master

Stuff You Need to Know

This activity can be easily adjusted to the age of your students. You may choose to start small and just section off part of your local park in order to preserve it or replant it with (forest) plant life you have collected (bee balm, mountain laurel, etc.). High school students can go the distance and work toward a much bigger and ambitious goal. Be inspired. Make a difference!

1. Discuss the Local Ecosystem

Discuss the local ecosystem, paying special attention to how it has changed over the last 50 years.

Here are some guiding questions:

- What animals were once there? What animals remain? Where have the animals gone?
- What has become of the local plant life?
- Is the local environment under stress or in danger from outside or inside forces, such as car exhaust, population pressure, new or old industry, mining, farming, or new housing?
- What can be done to help preserve the environment/animal life?
  - Are there new species of plants and animals in the ecosystem? How did they get there?

2. Contact Local Environmental Groups

Have a speaker talk about preservation and conservation. This person will serve as your advisor and possible leader.

The Dramatically Different Classroom • Christine Laitta & Mark Weakland
Kagan Publishing • 1 (800) WEE CO-OP • www.KaganOnline.com

3. Students Create a Plan of Action

Brainstorm a list of stresses on the environment and discuss problems that may appear or are happening right now. Pay special attention to wild or natural areas that may be threatened by development or areas that were destroyed. Generate a list of possible solutions that have been identified within the community. Is it possible to preserve a natural area or reintroduce natural plants and/or animals into an area that currently lacks them? With the aid of the teacher and/or a local activist, write a plan/proposal and submit it to the appropriate authorities.

4. Create a Petition

Along with your proposal send along a list of signatures. This shows the commitment and support of the class.

5. Chart Evidence

In addition to the petition, send graphs that chart your discoveries and concerns. Also think about using video. Video is very concrete and can sway the viewer.

6. Scale Model

Students work together to create a scale model and drawings of their newly restored area or nature preserve. This is then used as a visual aid for their oral presentation to their audience.

Enhancers

• Challenge students to become "experts." After finding additional information on the problem, they can prepare their own speeches to be presented to the decision makers.
• Videotape several speeches.

Multiple Intelligences

• Verbal/Linguistic
• Visual/Spatial
• Bodily/Kinesthetic
• Interpersonal
• Logical/Mathematical
• Naturalist

The Dramatically Different Classroom • Christine Laitta & Mark Weakland
Kagan Publishing • 1 (800) WEE CO-OP • www.KaganOnline.com

161

Local Ecosystem Review

Group members _____

1. How has the ecosystem changed over the years?

_____

_____

_____

_____

2. What animals were once there? What animals remain? Where have the animals gone?

_____

_____

_____

_____

_____

3. What has become of the local plant life?

_____

_____

_____

_____

_____

4. Is the local environment under stress or in danger from outside or inside forces such as car exhaust, population pressure, new or old industry, mining, farming, or new housing?

_____

_____

_____

_____

The Dramatically Different Classroom · Christine Laitta & Mark Weakland
Kagan Publishing · 1 (800) WEE CO-OP · www.KaganOnline.com

Local Ecosystem Review

5. What can be done to help preserve the environment/animal life?

_____

_____

_____

_____

6. Are there new species of plants and animals in the ecosystem? How did they get there?

_____

_____

_____

_____

Draw a picture of how you would protect the plants and animals of the ecosystem.

The Dramatically Different Classroom • Christine Laitta & Mark Weakland
Kagan Publishing • 1 (800) WEE CO-OP • www.KaganOnline.com

163

Conservation Action Plan

Name_____

☐ Learn about and discuss the natural environment of your geographic area. Learn what it was like 100 years ago and 50 years ago, and what it is like today.

☐ Identify natural areas in your community that are in danger of being destroyed and natural areas that have already been damaged or destroyed.

☐ Consult with and learn from another adult who is an expert in conservation and natural resources.

☐ Working with a group of students, draw up a proposal for saving a natural area or returning a damaged area to a more natural state.

☐ Create a petition that states your mission and proposal. Have others sign the petition.

☐ Work to become an expert on the natural resources and environment of your community. Do your own research and share what you have learned with others. You may want to make a graph, write a report, or create a video.

☐ With the aid of the teacher and/or a local activist, submit your proposal and the petition to the appropriate authorities.

☐ With a group of students, create a scale model of your proposed solution to a community environmental problem.

☐ Share your information, proposal, and scale model with other teachers and students.

The Dramatically Different Classroom • Christine Laitta & Mark Weakland
Kagan Publishing • 1 (800) WEE CO-OP • www.KaganOnline.com

Only Skin Deep

Students become a live model of the skin by taking on characteristics of each skin layer. After becoming cells in the epidermis, sweat glands, and hair follicles, students will be "itching" to do this activity again.

1. Review

Read about and discuss the form and function of the skin's layers.

2. Your Epidermis Is Showing

Have students sit in a line of five (depending upon the size of your class) parallel to the front of the class. They represent the epidermis.

3. Form the Dermis

The second line kneels behind the first, facing their backs. They are the dermis.

4. Form the Subcutaneous Tissue

The third line, which is the subcutaneous tissue, should be two or three students standing very close to one another with elbows linked. This represents the space that fat takes up.

5. Hair It Is

Space students between the layers of the skin. Have them raise their arms above their heads to represent hair. Their arms should be very straight and their palms should be pressed together. These students are the hair follicles.

6. Add the Sweat Glands

Space students between the layers of the skin to make sweat glands. (There is a lot of humor in this step, but we manage to rise above it!). One arm should be raised and fingers should be moving. This represents perspiration being given off.

7. Add the Capillaries

Capillaries are represented by students who stretch and contract their arms and legs depending on what the temperature it is.

8. Pose Environmental Questions

The teacher takes on the role of the environment and gives questions to the skin, such as "I'm a hot ray of sun shining down you. How are you going to protect the body, skin?"

Stuff You Need

• A picture of a cross section of the human skin (Yuck, Gross!)
• A large, clear space

Stuff You Need to Know

Transforming book information into a live model requires that students have an understanding of the functions of each skin layer.

Enhancers

• Use props. Feathers in the hands can be hair, a little cup of water can help the sweat glands give off moisture, and a jacket that can be put on and taken off helps represent the capillaries reacting to temperature.

Multiple Intelligences

• Verbal/Linguistic
• Interpersonal
• Visual/Spatial
• Bodily/Kinesthetic
• Naturalist

The Dramatically Different Classroom • Christine Laitta & Mark Weakland
Kagan Publishing • 1 (800) WEE CO-OP • www.KaganOnline.com

165

Digestion: The Inside Story

Students become human digestive organs and learn the specific functions of each organ as well as their interrelationships. In addition to bringing the workings of the digestive system to light and promoting ensemble, the movements of this activity help students "digest" digestion facts and vocabulary.

Stuff You Need

• A space to get the students on their feet

Stuff You Need to Know

In this activity, students learn by doing. Once again the abstract becomes concrete. The teacher may also want to address nutrition during this lesson.

1. The Food Pyramid

Introduce the food pyramid and discuss the ratio of the food groups to one another.

2. Sandwich Building

At their desks, have students make a nutritious but imaginary sandwich based on the food groups. It can have unusual combinations, like apple and turkey, as long as it is healthy. Have them share what their sandwich is made of. Then they all take an imaginary bite.

3. Discussing the Esophagus

The teacher asks the class "where do you think the food went?" Explaining that she will play the role of the food, she tells the class the first destination is the esophagus.

4. Becoming the Esophagus

A group of students form a circle to create the esophagus. It can expand or contract when the students step away from or toward the middle. The teacher is in the center of the circle pretending to slide down the esophagus.

The Dramatically Different Classroom • Christine Laitta & Mark Weakland
Kagan Publishing • 1 (800) WEE CO-OP • www.KaganOnline.com

5. Becoming the Stomach

Form the stomach by having the same students sit on the floor in their circle. They pound the floor with their fists to pound the imaginary food. They can also pantomime tearing the food into little bits. The teacher is in the center of the stomach slowly becoming smaller and smaller. Soon the food becomes a soupy mess.

6. Becoming the Small Intestine

Create the small intestine by pairing students, London Bridge style, in a big, long line. Students sing "nutrients are taken out, taken out, taken out" to the tune of *London Bridge* as the teacher walks under their arms.

7. Becoming the Large Intestine

To make the large intestine, the students remain in their London Bridge formation, but take a step away from their partner so that the tube is fatter. The teacher walks through the tube as the students sing "water now is taken out, taken out, taken out, water now is taken out, all that's left is waste."

Enhancers

• Act out the pulmonary system, circulatory, and/or muscular systems.

Multiple Intelligences

• Verbal/Linguistic
• Interpersonal
• Visual/Spatial
• Bodily/Kinesthetic
• Musical/Rhythmic
• Naturalist

The Dramatically Different Classroom • Christine Laitta & Mark Weakland
Kagan Publishing • 1 (800) WEE CO-OP • www.KaganOnline.com

167

Hygiene: The Whole Dirty Story

Students become the germs they come in contact with every day. You should see a lot more hand washing after this activity!

Stuff You Need

- A clear space
- Label-making materials, tape, markers, and paper for the children who will be germs
- String or yarn to tie from wrist to wrist or a belt buckle to connect the germs to their carrier
- Chain of Germs blackline master

Stuff You Need to Know

Hygiene is a difficult concept to teach because it is invisible—you can't see germs! This activity helps make hygiene real because it lets students see all of the germs they come in contact with and collect on any given day.

1. Talk About Germs

Discuss how germs are carried and how they affect people and their health.

2. Select Your Characters

Ask for two volunteers to portray people in the play *A Day in the Life of Germs.* These are the characters that come in contact with germs.

3. Generate Ideas for a Story Line

The class generates a list of daily activities, such as talking on the phone, going to school, eating lunch, using the bathroom, playing outside, etc., and uses it as a reference when telling the story.

4. Identify Germs

Explain to the rest of the class that they will be the germs. As the play progresses, the class sees situations that might bring the main characters into contact with germs. When this happens, the class says "Germ Alert" and then one student becomes that specific germ.

The Dramatically Different Classroom • Christine Laitta & Mark Weakland
Kagan Publishing • 1 (800) WEE CO-OP • www.KaganOnline.com

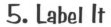

5. Label It

Make a label that describes where that germ was born. For example, the teacher may say the following as she makes up a story: "Mary was eating her breakfast and she sneezed into her hand!" The students say "Germ Alert" and one student makes a label that says "sneeze in the hand."

6. Germs and Their Life Journey

When a germ situation occurs, a germ or germs from the class (with a label) attach themselves to one or both of the two main characters in the story. This illustrates how germs stay with a person. As the students continue to act out their day, the germs stay with them and the chain gets bigger as the story continues.

7. Eliminating Germs

When students wash their hands, the chain can be cut.

8. Tell the Story

The teacher can read from a premade story or simply improvise it in class. Watch those germs pile up!

9. Chain of Germs

Have students fill out the Chain of Germs blackline and share them with another pair.

The Dramatically Different Classroom • Christine Laitta & Mark Weakland
Kagan Publishing • 1 (800) WEE CO-OP • www.KaganOnline.com

169

Chain of Germs

Name_____

Directions: Create a chain of germs that could attach to your hands or to your body throughout the day. Tell how you might pick up the germs and where the germs would attach. At the end of the sheet, tell how you would get rid of the germs!

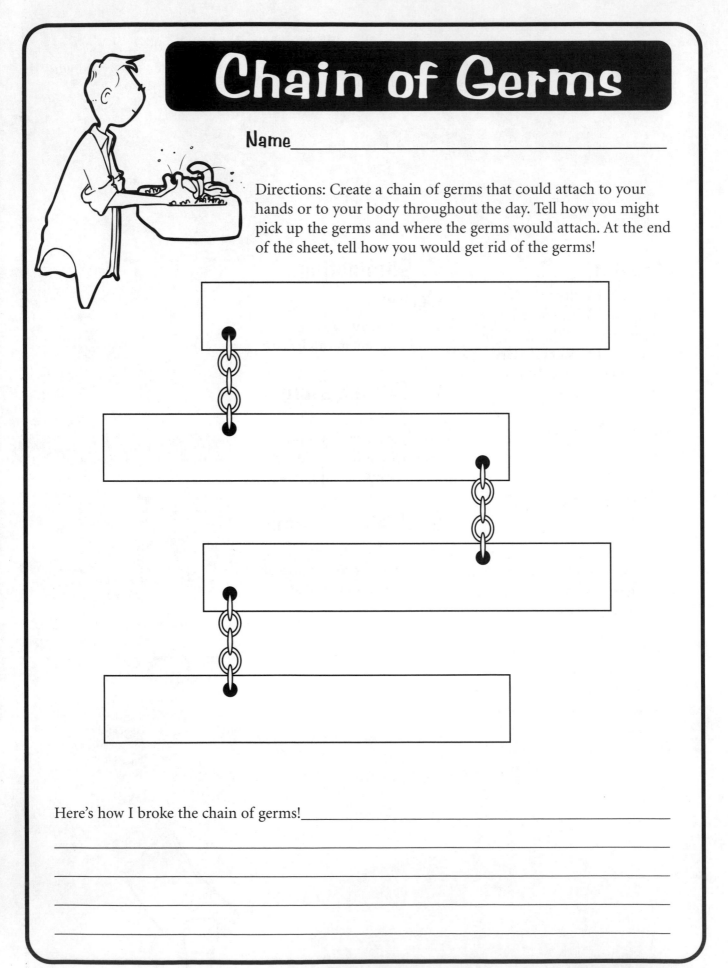

Here's how I broke the chain of germs!_____

_____

_____

_____

_____

The Dramatically Different Classroom • Christine Laitta & Mark Weakland
Kagan Publishing • 1 (800) WEE CO-OP • www.KaganOnline.com

Diseases: Spreading the Truth

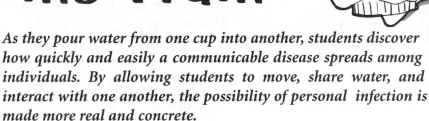

As they pour water from one cup into another, students discover how quickly and easily a communicable disease spreads among individuals. By allowing students to move, share water, and interact with one another, the possibility of personal infection is made more real and concrete.

1. Health and Personal Safety Discussion

Each school has its own curriculum on the mechanics and prevention of communicable diseases. Discuss the AIDS virus or a sexually transmitted disease within the parameters of your school's curriculum.

2. Demonstrate the Litmus Paper

Demonstrate to the class how litmus paper works. Show that it does not react to plain tap water, but it does change color when placed in contact with an acid.

3. Fill Up and "Infect" the Cups

Every student is given a paper or plastic cup filled half full with water. The teacher explains that the water represents each person's body fluids. The teacher then "infects" two of the students by pouring an acidic liquid such as vinegar (that will change the color of litmus paper) into his or her cup. If litmus paper is not available this activity can be done using food coloring.

4. Share the Water

Each student in the room is responsible for finding three other students and pouring a bit of his or her liquid into the other's cup. When each student has shared "body fluids" with three others, the entire class tests the results by dipping a piece of litmus paper into each cup.

5. Class Discussion

Discuss the discovered rate of infection and the ease at which infectious diseases are spread.

Stuff You Need

- Paper or plastic cups (one per student)
- Pitcher of water
- Litmus paper (one strip per student)
- An acidic liquid, such as vinegar

Stuff You Need to Know

This activity provides the teacher with an easy way of adapting a sensitive topic to the health class.

Enhancers

- Take data on the rate of infection. Generate graphs that are based on the data.
- Have groups of students work together to create a plan that makes suggestions for stopping or slowing the rate of infection.

Multiple Intelligences

- Verbal Linguistic
- Interpersonal
- Visual/Spatial
- Bodily/Kinesthetic
- Intrapersonal
- Naturalist

The Dramatically Different Classroom • Christine Laitta & Mark Weakland
Kagan Publishing • 1 (800) WEE CO-OP • www.KaganOnline.com

171

Safety Hero

Students learn safety rules by singing songs, playing games, listening to stories, and correcting the teacher when he or she does something dangerous. This activity teaches rules of the road, bike safety, and how to identify signs and danger zones, and is designed so older students can teach safety to younger siblings and children in day-care centers. This activity promotes community service, volunteerism, and safety.

Stuff You Need

- Materials to represent cars
- Masking tape to create sidewalks, driveways, and crosswalks
- A traffic light
- The following signs: stop, yield, walk, don't walk, school crossing, safe home, traffic, and construction site.
- Safety Hero blackline master

Stuff You Need to Know

This activity happens in several stages. The more realistic the staging area, the greater the impact. Contact your local art teacher who may be able to help with the creating of signs and a traffic signal. Once the students become safety heroes, they graduate to helping and teaching others who are younger or learning challenged. Also contact your local police, who are usually more than willing to come and speak.

1. Create the Safety Zone

In the class, gym, or playground, create a street scene including cars, driveways, sidewalks, crosswalks, a traffic light, and safety signs. Sit students on the ground. (Do not sit them in the middle of your "street.") Students should be able to clearly see the street and all of the props, obstacles, cars, and signs.

2. Survey Students

Survey the group to find out what they already know about safety. Congratulate students for their contributions. Explain to the group that today they are going to become "Safety Heroes." Ask students what they think a Safety Hero does. Tell the group a Safety Hero is a person who teaches others all they know about safety.

3. Sing the Safety Hero Theme

Create your own melody or rap and motions for the Safety Hero blackline master.

4. Identify the Danger Zones

Form groups of four. Have groups discuss the possible danger zones. Now the groups walk through the "street" and place their danger zone identification cards where they feel a person may get hurt. The term danger zone should be used regularly to remind students to stay alert.

The Dramatically Different Classroom · Christine Laitta & Mark Weakland
Kagan Publishing • 1 (800) WEE CO-OP • www.KaganOnline.com

5. Discuss the Students' Choices

Now have the class travel to each danger zone that is identified with a card. Ask groups why they consider that spot a danger zone.

6. Sing

Sing your safety song again.

7. Safety Walk

Walk your safety zone. Have students follow along and give advice as you encounter potential hazards. Pose safety questions and encourage students to create several different solutions before choosing the best solution (which may be a combination of ideas).

- **Teacher:** "I have to cross the street so I can visit my friend. What do I do?"
- **Student 1:** "Ask an older sibling or parent to cross with you."
- **Student 2:** "Look both ways and then run."
- **Student 3:** "Use the crosswalk."
- **Student 4:** "Hold a grown-up's hand."

Now discuss how the teacher can incorporate all of the safe and helpful ideas into her solution. Point out any ideas that are not safe.

- **Teacher:** "I think I will ask my dad to hold my hand and cross the street with me in the crosswalk. I don't think running is a safe idea because I could trip and fall."

Here are more safety questions to ask students:

- How do I get off the school bus and cross in front of it?
- I want to ride my bike over to my friend's house.
- What do I do if I see orange cones marking off an area?
- What do I do if I see a flashing "Don't Walk" sign and I've already started to cross?

Enhancers

- Create a commercial that advertises Safety Heroes
- Get a school bus and practice the following: getting on and off, crossing in front, sitting no more than two in a seat, proper placement of books, where to place your hands, speaking in a whisper, and many other safety rules you can discover.
- List all of the things a bus driver needs to pay attention to.
- This lesson is intended to be helpful for all ages. This is a wonderful community service project for high school students who may want to teach others or an activity for an early childhood development class. It can also be an outreach project/play to take to elementary schools.

Multiple Intelligences

- Verbal/Linguistic
- Interpersonal
- Visual/Spatial
- Bodily/Kinesthetic
- Intrapersonal
- Musical/Rhythmic
- Logical/Mathematical

The Dramatically Different Classroom • Christine Laitta & Mark Weakland
Kagan Publishing • 1 (800) WEE CO-OP • www.KaganOnline.com

173

Safety Hero (Continued)

8. Students Become Teachers

Empower students to teach you a safety lesson by calling, "Freeze" every time you do something dangerous. Thank students and have them share what you were doing wrong and what you should do. Tell students they must watch closely because at any time you may do something unsafe. For example, while you are telling them this, slowly start backing off the designated curb into the street. As you walk around the town, point out places and things you enjoy while simultaneously doing unsafe things. Here are some suggestions:

- "Over here is where I enjoy reading." (as you walk cross the street without looking)
- "This is my friend's car. It's fun to play around." (push the car up and down)
- "This is my driveway where I like to Rollerblade." (throw rocks into the street)
- "This is where I like to play pirates." (kick over or lean on construction cones)
- "This is where my bus picks me up." (start a game of tag by the street)
- "This is my bus. I love to check out all the stuff on it." (grab a mirror and begin to adjust it)

9. Sing

Sing the song again.

10. Safety Tales

The teacher and students sit in a circle. Students listen to stories told by either their teacher or another student and shout out "Freeze" when they hear unsafe behavior. Students then identify the behavior and give a safe solution. This increases listening comprehension and verbal skills. Here is an example:

- "I woke up this morning and I was so excited because it was my birthday. So, I ran down the steps (freeze) tore open my present, throwing the wrapping paper everywhere (freeze), and put on my new Rollerblades (freeze). I had to skate up the street to my best friend's house (freeze) I skated as fast as I could and..."

Here's a list of the unsafe behaviors within the story:

- Running down steps
- Throwing paper on the steps where someone could slide on it
- Wearing Rollerblades in the house
- No helmet, pads
- Did not tell parents you were leaving or where you were going
- Skated in the street
- And for those who were really listening, she never put on any clothes, never brushed her teeth, or thanked her parents for the great gift.

The Dramatically Different Classroom • Christine Laitta & Mark Weakland
Kagan Publishing • 1 (800) WEE CO-OP • www.KaganOnline.com

Safety Hero (Continued)

11. Crossing the Street

As the teacher stands in the middle of the crosswalk, have a student hold the hand of a classmate and cross the street. Remind them to walk with a purpose. No running, no strolling, and no daydreaming. Remind students to check both ways the entire time they are crossing. No flicking your head so quickly you don't see anything.

12. Review the Signs

Have the group sit in a circle and show them various street signs. Discuss what they mean and where you would find them. To test students' comprehension, have them create poems, songs, or skits about the signs.

13. Student Safety Heroes

Create a ceremony in which the students become "Safety Heroes." Try writing a pledge and passing out certificates and/or badges. Remind students that as Safety Heroes they must teach safety rules to others younger then themselves. End the ceremony by singing your Safety Hero song.

The Dramatically Different Classroom • Christine Laitta & Mark Weakland
Kagan Publishing • 1 (800) WEE CO-OP • www.KaganOnline.com

175

Safety Hero Theme Song

You gotta stop, look, and listen
You gotta listen, look, and stop
Safety street is where we learn the rules that help us lots

Holdin' hands is always best 'stead of crossin all alone
When we see a broken window, we call that a danger zone

You gotta stop, look, and listen
You gotta listen, look, and stop
Safety street is where we learn the rules that help us lots

When you're feelin' kinda nervous, 'cause there's someone botherin' you
A policeman's there to help and he'll know just what to do

When you're ridin' your bike and gotta get across that street
Don't be a fool, get off, use your feet

You gotta stop, look, and listen
You gotta listen, look, and stop
Be a safety hero and you will always rock

The Dramatically Different Classroom • Christine Laitta & Mark Weakland
Kagan Publishing • 1 (800) WEE CO-OP • www.KaganOnline.com

Building the Food Pyramid

Students become the food pyramid by creating costumes and building the food pyramid with their bodies. They also learn food facts and nutritional information.

1. Review the Food Pyramid

Have students review the foods that make up the pyramid and the quantities they need to consume if they want to eat a balanced diet. Use a picture of the pyramid as a reference.

2. Cast Your Food Characters

Assign each student a food from each of the food groups. Make sure you divide the class so you have enough students for each level of the pyramid.

3. Students Research Their Food

Once the students know their food, give them time to gather information. Encourage them to bring in and share their food with the class. Have them find facts on how the food is beneficial to someone who is sick and someone who is healthy.

4. Create a Costume

Have students dress themselves to represent their food. For example, have a student dress in all orange and wear a green hat to represent a carrot.

5. Create the Pyramid

Have some students sit in a line on the floor. A second line kneels behind the first, facing their backs. The third line sits in chairs and the fourth line stands. Remember that the base of the pyramid uses more students and only one or two should be standing at the top.

Stuff You Need

- Chairs
- Facts on the specific foods in the food pyramid
- A picture of the food pyramid

Stuff You Need to Know

By becoming the foods in the pyramid, students are encouraged to establish a healthy diet.

Enhancers

- Take a photo of the pyramid.
- How about a food pyramid formed on a moving bicycle, like the Chinese acrobats?

Multiple Intelligences

- Verbal/Linguistic
- Interpersonal
- Visual/Spatial
- Bodily/Kinesthetic
- Intrapersonal
- Naturalist

The Dramatically Different Classroom • Christine Laitta & Mark Weakland
Kagan Publishing • 1 (800) WEE CO-OP • www.KaganOnline.com

177

Taking a Break
(Enough Already!)

The Dramatically Different Classroom • Christine Laitta & Mark Weakland
Kagan Publishing • 1 (800) WEE CO-OP • www.KaganOnline.com

179

Do a Little Dance

Students get out of their seats to do a little dance and have a little fun. This activity is a stress reliever and a fun reward for a job well done, and it promotes musicality, self-expression, and self-confidence through the use of the body.

Stuff You Need

• CD player and/or tape player
• A selection of music on CD or tape
• A clear space to move in
• Five minutes

Stuff You Need to Know

Before and after a test students are tense, nervous, and worried. Try introducing a dance break to free up the mind, get the blood flowing, and have fun. Encourage students to get out of their seats to wiggle, sing, and dance. Don't forget to set up the boundaries; students will play and stay in control when they understand the rules. The music provides classroom management. Use calm and soft music when you want to create this type of atmosphere. Turn down the volume of the music to let the group know when the activity is coming to an end.

Enhancers

• Create a class dance.
• Do an already established dance such as the Hokey Pokey or the Electric Slide.

Multiple Intelligences

• Musical/Rhythmic
• Bodily/Kinesthetic

1. Set Aside Five Minutes

Create a five minute break in your day.

2. Set the Rules

Before you begin, set the boundaries. These may change depending on the age and temperament of your students.

• As the teacher fades down the music, the students must bring the dance to a close.
• Remind students that when the music ends it is their job to refocus and return to their work space.
• Depending on the age and maturity of students, they may want to do a partner dance, such as the twist or the polka, or they may want to keep to their own space.

3. Clean and Clear

Make sure the area is clear. Have students put away their work, pencils, and slide rules!

4. Dance

Dance and have fun.

5. Finish the Dance

Fade the volume and allow the students to refocus.

The Dramatically Different Classroom • Christine Laitta & Mark Weakland
Kagan Publishing • 1 (800) WEE CO-OP • www.KaganOnline.com

Eraser Tag

Classroom ensemble is promoted as students "run" a relay around an established classroom path with erasers on their heads. The team that finishes first wins. When and if the eraser falls off someone's head, the student begins again.

1. Set Your Relay Course

Have students follow you through the maze of desks.

2. Group the Teams

Depending on the size of your class, group students into teams and line them up in a relay formation one behind the other.

3. Create the Rules

Create rules for the game.
- If the eraser falls off the player's head, he or she must return to the beginning.
- To pass the eraser from player to player, the person who is doing the handoff must place it on the next player's head.
- No running.

Stuff You Need

- An eraser for each relay team

Stuff You Need to Know

You may want to clean the erasers before you place them on students' heads or you may not! The energy level is kept in check because students must limit their body movements in order to keep the erasers on their heads. Be aware that students with flatter heads will have an unfair advantage over those with round heads!

Enhancers

- Try using other classroom objects, such as books (or slide rules)!
- Play the game outside.

Multiple Intelligences

- Bodily/Kinesthetic
- Interpersonal

The Dramatically Different Classroom • Christine Laitta & Mark Weakland
Kagan Publishing • 1 (800) WEE CO-OP • www.KaganOnline.com

181

You Have Changed

After memorizing the appearance of a partner, students try to fool each other by changing their appearance, attitude, and/or posture. This activity promotes concentration and memorization, and it's fun!

Stuff You Need

• A clear space

Stuff You Need to Know

This is the type of activity that may be found in a resource room.

Note from the Author:
As a former student of a learning support program, I loved playing these memory games because I saw my ability to memorize and concentrate improve rapidly… Now, where was I?

Enhancers

• Try using several people.
• Try having two teams play. The team decides which things will be changed. This is much more difficult. Teams should take time to discuss what they think has changed and then agree upon an answer.

Multiple Intelligences

• Bodily/Kinesthetic
• Verbal/Linguistic
• Visual/Spatial
• Interpersonal

1. Pair Up

Students choose a partner they haven't worked with and find a place to move and play.

2. Study Your Partner

Have students take time to observe their partner. Remind students they will need to take a mental picture of their partner's facial expressions and how their partner is dressed and/or standing.

3. Change Yourself

Have students turn their backs to each other and change three things about themselves. Students can untuck their shirts, cuff their pants, change their attitude, and change their voice. The list goes on.

4. You Have Changed

Students face each other and guess what is different about each other.

The Dramatically Different Classroom • Christine Laitta & Mark Weakland
Kagan Publishing • 1 (800) WEE CO-OP • www.KaganOnline.com

Lanterns

Students make and display lanterns out of recycled 2-liter bottles. Using tissue paper and their own designs, students create a work of self-expression.

1. Recycle

Have your students bring in their old 2-liter containers until you have one for each student.

2. Choose Your Theme

Have students choose their designs and select the materials they will need. For example, if they are creating a stained-glass effect, they will need many different colors of tissue paper and a black magic marker.

3. Cover Your Bottle in Glue

Have students cover the surface with glue and then begin pasting the tissue paper onto the container.

4. Add On

Make sure students put on enough layers of tissue paper. Remind them to keep covering the paper with the glue so it will stay attached to the bottle.

5. Let It Dry

Set aside an area for the lanterns to dry.

6. Punch Holes

Punch holes on either side of the 2-liter bottle that are big enough to string the lights through.

7. Light the Lanterns

Collect a string of twinkle lights and string up your lanterns

Stuff You Need

- A 2-liter bottle (one for each student). You will need to cut the necks off!
- Colored tissue paper cut into shapes
- Watered-down glue in small containers (one per student)
- Paint brushes

Stuff You Need to Know

This is a wonderful activity that a student can work on a little each day. Make sure your watered-down glue is in an airtight container.

Enhancers

- After reading or writing a classroom story, allow students to retell it through the lanterns. Each student will design a specific image or event from the story. String the lanterns in chronological order.

Multiple Intelligences

- Bodily/Kinesthetic
- Visual/Spatial

The Dramatically Different Classroom • Christine Laitta & Mark Weakland
Kagan Publishing • 1 (800) WEE CO-OP • www.KaganOnline.com

183

Scavenger Hunt

Students search for hidden objects that the teacher has placed in and around the classroom. This is a great rainy day/snowy day activity, even for middle school students.

Stuff You Need

- A list of items that students need to find (one list per student)
- Several interesting items (to be hidden)

Stuff You Need to Know

This activity can be done outside or with small groups of students, and can be as long and as difficult as you choose.

Enhancers

- Have students search for things that can be recycled.
- Give students several days to collect things.
- Create clues to lead students in the right direction.
- Have students search for things relating to their topic of study.

Multiple Intelligences

- Bodily/Kinesthetic
- Logical/Mathematical

1. Choose Your Items

Choose a group of objects and hide them in and around your classroom. If you are able to do this outside, you can have students find four-leaf clovers, specific plants and trees and much more.

2. Students Search

Have students search, either independently or in groups, for the hidden items.

3. Seek and Ye Shall Find

Have students return and reveal what they have found.

The Dramatically Different Classroom • Christine Laitta & Mark Weakland
Kagan Publishing • 1 (800) WEE CO-OP • www.KaganOnline.com

7-Up

Students place their heads on the desk, close their eyes, and keep their thumbs up and out. Seven other students are the tappers. They tiptoe around the room and tap the thumb of one of their classmates. The students who were tapped must guess who tapped them.

1. Choose Your 7-Up

Choose seven students to stand in front of the class.

2. Lights Off, Thumbs Up

Turn off the lights. Students put their heads down and their thumbs up. No peeking. The seven students each tap one other student. That student places his or her thumb down so he or she is not tapped again.

3. The Lights Are Turned Back On

Now the students whose thumbs were tapped must figure out who was the tapper.

4. Switch

When students guess correctly, they replace the tapper and become one of the seven up.

Stuff You Need

• Thumbs

Stuff You Need to Know

Students may try choosing their friends over and over, so do not allow students to choose the same person more than once.

Multiple Intelligences

• Bodily/Kinesthetic
• Logical/Mathematical
• Interpersonal

The Dramatically Different Classroom • Christine Laitta & Mark Weakland
Kagan Publishing • 1 (800) WEE CO-OP • www.KaganOnline.com

185

Who's the Leader?

After one student leaves the group, the rest of the class chooses a person to be it. This person starts a motion that the rest of the group follows. The person chosen continuously changes the motions while the others follow. Meanwhile, the removed person rejoins the group, stands in the middle, and guesses who the leader is.

Stuff You Need

• A place for the group to sit in a circle

Stuff You Need to Know

The leader must change the movements frequently in order to keep the game moving and make it fair.

Enhancers

• Try it with sounds.

Multiple Intelligences

• Interpersonal
• Bodily/Kinesthetic
• Visual/Spatial
• Logical/Mathematical

1. Circle Up

Have the class sit on the floor in a large circle.

2. Choose a Student

The teacher picks a student to stand outside the door or behind a screen. Meanwhile, the group chooses a leader.

3. Begin the Movements

Students begin to follow the leader. The student sent outside then joins the group. He or she stands in the center of the class circle.

4. Figure It Out

The student in the center has three guesses to figure out who is leading. If he or she doesn't figure out who the leader is, the leader must reveal him or herself.

5. Switch

Have the leader (or someone else) be the guesser.

The Dramatically Different Classroom • Christine Laitta & Mark Weakland
Kagan Publishing • 1 (800) WEE CO-OP • www.KaganOnline.com

Who Am I?

In this role-playing activity, students are guests at a party and take on the persona of famous figures in history, favorite celebrities, or cartoon characters. The host of the party asks the guests indirect questions in order to figure out who the guests are.

1. Pick Party Guests

Have each student select a well-known or recently studied character. Students do a short character study including reviewing his or her character's likes, hobbies, age, schooling, family, movements, habits, attitudes, major achievements, and so on.

2. Choose a Host

You can have more than one host. Give them a time limit in which to figure out who has come to their party.

Stuff You Need

• A large clear space

Stuff You Need to Know

The guest needs to give a lot of creative hints and the host needs to use creative questioning techniques in order to discover who the party guest is. For example, a guest scratches at the door. The host opens the door and the guest begins sniffing the food. Host: "Would you like a dog biscuit to go with those chips?" Guest (growling loudly) "No!" Guest rubs himself against a wall (much like a bear would do). Host: "Would you like honey on those chips, Mr. Bear?" (This is the identity of the guest—a good guess!).

Multiple Intelligences

• Bodily/Kinesthetic
• Verbal/Linguistic
• Visual/Spatial
• Logical/Mathematical
• Interpersonal

The Dramatically Different Classroom • Christine Laitta & Mark Weakland
Kagan Publishing • 1 (800) WEE CO-OP • www.KaganOnline.com

187

Improvisation With Specific Words

Students are given three pieces of paper. On one piece they write a person, on another a place, and on the last piece a thing. Students select one piece from each separate pile and create a short scenario to act out. In this activity, students develop verbal skills as well as exercise their creative thinking and problem-solving skills.

Stuff You Need

• Slips of paper (three slips per student)
• A bowl, hat, or box to keep the paper in
• A clear space to move in

Stuff You Need to Know

This activity can be done in small groups or individually. Students should be given a short time (approximately two minutes) to create and practice their story.

Multiple Intelligences

• Verbal/Linguistic
• Logical/Mathematical
• Bodily/Linguistic
• Visual/Spatial

1. Pass Out Paper

Give each student three pieces of paper.

2. Generate Ideas

Students write down a person, a place, and a thing, one for each piece of paper, and then place them in the corresponding pile in the front of the room.

3. Pick a Piece of Paper

After the teacher shuffles each pile, the students select a slip of paper from each pile.

4. Create a Scenario

Either in groups or individually, students come up with stories that fit the pieces of paper.

5. Act It Out

Have students share their stories with the class. Have the class guess what was on the three pieces of paper.

The Dramatically Different Classroom • Christine Laitta & Mark Weakland
Kagan Publishing • 1 (800) WEE CO-OP • www.KaganOnline.com

Class TV

Students make a video to one of their favorite songs.

1. Choose Your Song

After the song is picked, students discuss all the possible stories that could be taking place.

2. Location Scout

Students decide where they would like to film the video. They may want to build their own set.

3. Cast It

With the help of the teacher, students assign their roles, either behind the camera or in front of the camera. Cast as many people as you want.

4. Write a Script

Create dialogue to go before and after the video. This will help to set the scene and establish characters. The teacher can either choose script writers or it can be a class activity.

5. Film It

Film it!

6. Watch It

Watch it!

Stuff You Need

- Storyboard or a place to map out the story line of the video
- A clear space
- Video equipment
- Props specific to the song

Stuff You Need to Know

This activity can be filmed on location or in the classroom. The video can be worked on a little bit each day, as time allows, but the actual filming will take a chunk of time. Ask the school's AV department for assistance and possible editing.

Enhancers

- Popcorn

Multiple Intelligences

- Bodily/Kinesthetic
- Interpersonal
- Visual/Spatial

The Dramatically Different Classroom • Christine Laitta & Mark Weakland
Kagan Publishing • 1 (800) WEE CO-OP • www.KaganOnline.com

189

Moving Music

The teacher plays music in order to signal transition times, such as moving from class to class or activity to activity. This activity promotes active listening and allows students to refocus and have time to prepare for the next class or activity. It also appeals to students' musical intelligence.

Stuff You Need

- A selection of music based on your daily transitions
- Cassette or CD player

Stuff You Need to Know

Many students need advance notice that transitions are coming and it is time to "switch gears." At any level, music can act as a transition helper and a management technique. Have music playing as students are entering the room. Experiment with different types, such as the latest *Red Hot Chili Peppers* or *Lauren Hill* tune, soothing ambient music, current jazz, or classical. When it is time for the class to begin, fade out the music. As students get ready to leave at the end of the period, give them a little time to listen before the next period begins.

Enhancers

- Have students select music to begin the day or any other transition.
- Arrange to have the music played over the school PA system.

Multiple Intelligences

- Musical/Rhythmic

I. Identify Transition Times

The teacher can use music as a cue that it is time to get ready for the next period or activity. At the end of two or three minutes of music, fade it out. Students should be quiet and ready to go by this time. Here are examples of transition times and some possibilities for musical selections.

Before AM classes start music:
- *A Little Night Music* by Mozart
- Beethoven's *Pastoral Symphony*

Before Gym Class Music:
- *Twist and Shout*
- *Do the Locomotion*

Before Lunch Music:
- *Mrs. Murphy's Chowder*
- *Eating Goober Peas*
- *Food, Glorious Food* from *Oliver*
- *Peanut Butter and Jelly*

Getting ready to go home music:
- *Country Roads* by John Denver
- *Feel Like I Gotta Travel On* by Traditional
- *So Long, It's Been Good to Know You* by Woody Guthrie

The Dramatically Different Classroom • Christine Laitta & Mark Weakland
Kagan Publishing • 1 (800) WEE CO-OP • www.KaganOnline.com

Bend & Stretch

Students take a little break, get a little exercise, and use their bodies when the teacher plays some prerecorded music or has the class sing.

1. The Time Is Right

This activity may work before that early morning high school physics class, before the after-lunch mathematics class, or during a long block.

2. The Perfect Music

What is right for the younger ones? *Bend and Stretch, Hokey Pokey, Father Abraham.* Sometimes you can cross over. In concert, Bobby McFerrin regularly does *Head and Shoulders* with his audience, and everyone, from five years old to fifty years old, loves it.

Rock/Pop Songs:
- Van Halen–*Jump*
- Frankie Valley and the Four Seasons–*Oh, What A Night*

Latest Dance:
- "Do the Locomotion"
- "The Electric Slide"
- "The Macarena"

3. Make Your Move

In order to develop trust, the teacher must shake his or her groove thing with the rest of the class. The teacher may be alone at first, but with repeated exposure, the whole class will be *Walkin' on Sunshine.*

Stuff You Need

- Selection of music
- A CD or cassette player

Stuff You Need to Know

From elementary students in a long language arts block to high school students in a long biology block, everyone needs a chance to get the blood flowing and the brain oxygenated. Sometimes students, especially elementary school boys or children with attention problems, get squirmy in their seats and need a chance to move a bit. This activity also acts as a great management technique. Make a contract that if the class completes a task, the teacher will play some great break music.

Enhancers

- Give extra credit points for students that come up with appropriate examples or a new group dance.

Multiple Intelligences

- Bodily/Kinesthetic
- Musical/Rhythmic
- Interpersonal

The Dramatically Different Classroom • Christine Laitta & Mark Weakland
Kagan Publishing • 1 (800) WEE CO-OP • www.KaganOnline.com

191

"Figure" It Out

Students use their bodies to create statues with strange combinations of body parts. While stretching, moving, and taking a break from the normal academic routine, students are also working on how to solve a problem and how to work as a team.

Stuff You Need

• Ideas for statues
• A clear space

Stuff You Need to Know

This activity requires a lot of body contact with other class members, so it is a good ice-breaker activity. Modify this activity based on the size of your class. You may want to split the class in half.

Enhancers

• Have students generate their own ideas for statues.

Multiple Intelligences

• Bodily/Kinesthetic
• Interpersonal
• Logical/Mathematical
• Visual/Spatial

1. Ideas for Statues

The teacher poses a problem to the class: "Create a statue, using every member of the class, with the following requirements: It must have twelve arms, seven legs on the ground, and ten heads," or "It must have two arms and twenty legs."

2. Solution

Remind students (if they get stuck) that the solution can sometimes be an obvious one. For example, the rest of the students can sit on chairs so that their feet are not touching the ground, they can link arms side by side with the two people on the ends sticking their arms out, or they can all stand on one foot!

The Dramatically Different Classroom • Christine Laitta & Mark Weakland
Kagan Publishing • 1 (800) WEE CO-OP • www.KaganOnline.com

Bibliography
(Useful info in ABC order)

Aardema, V. and Dillon, L.D.
Why Mosquitoes Buzz in Peoples' Ears.
Dial Books for Young Readers.

Abramson, R.M.
Rhythm games for perception and cognition.
Pittsburgh, PA: Volkwein Brothers, 1973.
Cassette and Book.

Anderson, Leroy.
The Leroy Anderson Collection.
MCA Special Markets, 1998.

Anderson, Marian.
He's Got the Whole World in His Hands–Spirituals.
BMG Classics, 1994.

Anderson, W.M. and Lawrence, J.E.
Integrating music into the classroom.
California: Wadsworth Publishing Company, 1991.

Blades, Ruben.
Buscando America.
Electra Entertainment, 1987.

Buffet, Jimmy.
Buffett Live: Tuesdays, Thursdays, Saturdays.
Mailboat Records, 1999.

Capra, Frank.
It's a Wonderful Life.
Republic Studios, 1946.

Coppola, Francis Ford.
Apocalypse Now.
Paramount Pictures, 1979.

Crosby, Stills, Nash, and Young.
Four Way Street.
Atlantic, 1971.

cummings, e.e.
100 Selected Poems.
Grove Press, 1989.

Dunn, S.
Crackers and crumbs: chants for whole language.
Portsmouth: Heinmann Educational Books, 1990.

Fleetwood Mac.
The Dance.
Warner Brothers, 1997.

Lee, Harper.
To Kill a Mockingbird.
Warner Books, Reissued 1988.

Hendrix, Jimi.
Live at Woodstock.
MCA, 1999.

Holtz, Gustav.
The Planets.
Deutche Grammaphone.

Johnson, David A.
Mother Hubbard: A Nursery Rhyme.
Margaret McElderry.

King Sunny Ade.
Live at the Hollywood Palace.
I.R.S. Records, 1994.

Led Zepplin.
Houses of the Holy.
Atlantic, 1973.

Lehrer, Tom.
Songs and More Songs by Tom Lehrer.
Atlantic/Rhino, 1997.

Kevin Locke.
Keepers of the Dream.
Earthbeat.

Marley, Ziggy.
Fallen Is Babylon.
Elektra Entertainment, 1997.

The Dramatically Different Classroom • Christine Laitta & Mark Weakland
Kagan Publishing • 1 (800) WEE CO-OP • www.KaganOnline.com

193

Miller, Arthur.
The Crucible: A Play in Four Acts.
Penguin, USA. 1953.

McDonald, D. and Simons, G.
Musical Growth and Development: Birth Through Six.
New York, NY: Schirmer Books, 1989.

Makeba, Mariam.
Sangoma.
1988.

Mitchell, Joni.
Clouds.
Warner Brothers, 1969.

Montgomery, Lucy Maud.
Anne of Green Gables.
New American Library, Reissued 1991.

Moody, W.J. (Ed.).
Artistic intelligences: implications for education.
New York, NY: Teachers College Press, 1990.

Morissette, Alanis.
Star Profile.
Mastertone, 1999.

Pfister, M. and James, J.A.
The Rainbow Fish.
North South Books, 1998.

Prelutsky, Jack.
The Dragons Are Singing Tonight.
Greenwillow, 1998.

Puente, Tito.
Tito Puente's Golden Latin Jazz All Stars.
RMM Records, 1992.

Rondstadt, Linda.
Canciones de Mi Padre (Songs of My Father).
Electra Entertainment, 1988.

Sendak, Maurice.
Chicken Soup With Rice.
Harper Trophy, 1962.

Silverstein, Shel.
A Light in the Attic.
Harpercollins Juvenile Books, 1981.

Siber, Irwin (Ed.).
Songs of the Civil War.
NY: Columbia University Press, 1960.

Sondheim, Steven.
Sunday in the Park With George.
Directed by James Lapine, with Bernadette Peters
and Mandy Patinkin, 1986.

The Baltimore Consort.
On the Banks of Helicon.
Dorian Recordings, 1990.

They Might Be Giants.
Flood.
Elektra Entertainment, 1990.

Weakland, Mark.
Rap it up: using rap rhythms to enhance learning.
CA: Academic Communications Associates, 1992.

Wells, H.G.
War of the Worlds.
(Audiocassette). Metacom, 1987.

Winter, Paul.
Common Ground.
A&M Records, 1978.

Wonder, Stevie.
Innervisions.
Motown, 1973.

Wood, Audrey and Don.
The Napping House.
Harcourt Brace, 1986.

194

The Dramatically Different Classroom • Christine Laitta & Mark Weakland
Kagan Publishing • 1 (800) WEE CO-OP • www.KaganOnline.com

Notes

The Dramatically Different Classroom • Christine Laitta & Mark Weakland
Kagan Publishing • 1 (800) WEE CO-OP • www.KaganOnline.com

195

Notes

The Dramatically Different Classroom · Christine Laitta & Mark Weakland
Kagan Publishing · 1 (800) WEE CO-OP · www.KaganOnline.com